"THE HIGHER CHRISTIAN LIFE"

SOURCES FOR THE STUDY OF THE HOLINESS, PENTECOSTAL, AND KESWICK MOVEMENTS

A forty-eight-volume facsimile series reprinting extremely rare documents for the study of nineteenth-century religious and social history, the rise of feminism, and the history of the Pentecostal and Charismatic movements

Edited by

Donald W. Dayton
Northern Baptist Theological Seminary

Advisory Editors

D. William Faupel, *Asbury Theological Seminary*
Cecil M. Robeck, Jr., *Fuller Theological Seminary*
Gerald T. Sheppard, *Union Theological Seminary*

A GARLAND SERIES

gle
sol
in
me,
of
e da
ad
that

ereste
d sa
the th
ng as
was a
of the
ght tha
at the j
trading
he Plant
Where a
premonit
n the dis
e still. C
Breakfast-t
friend, Di
steel. W
morning
wenty-seven
an intereste
ne-dogs after a
eached as usu
f engagements. Eve
nother cycle of usef
the one just closed

TWENTY-FIVE WONDERFUL YEARS
1889–1914
A POPULAR SKETCH OF THE CHRISTIAN AND MISSIONARY ALLIANCE

G. P. Pardington

Garland Publishing, Inc.
New York & London
1984

BX
6700
.A4
P37
1984

For a complete list of the titles in this series
see the final pages of this volume.

This facsimile has been made from a copy in
the Owosso College Library.

Library of Congress Cataloging in Publication Data

Pardington, G. P.
    Twenty-five wonderful years, 1889–1914.

    ("The Higher Christian life")
    Reprint. Originally published: New York City :
    Christian Alliance Pub. Co., c1914.
    1. Christian and Missionary Alliance—History.
    I. Title.   II. Series.
    BX6700.A4P37   1984   289.9   84-18832
        ISBN 0-8240-6435-6 (alk. paper)

The volumes in this series are printed on
acid-free, 250-year-life paper.

Printed in the United States of America

REV. A. B. SIMPSON.

Twenty-five Wonderful Years

1889—1914

A Popular Sketch

of the

CHRISTIAN AND MISSIONARY ALLIANCE

By

REV. G. P. PARDINGTON, PH. D.

✖

CHRISTIAN ALLIANCE PUBLISHING CO.
692 Eighth Avenue
New York City

To

Rev. and Mrs. A. B. Simpson

Whose lives of Faith, Love and Sacrifice

are interwoven with these

Twenty-five Wonderful Years

this volume is

respectfully and affectionately inscribed

TABLE OF CONTENTS

PREFACE.

A brief word of explanation on two points is due from the writer to his readers.

First, with one or two notable exceptions, no reference has been made to the part played in the history by living workers, either in the Homeland or in the Foreign Field. This omission has been intentional. The writer yields to no one in love of his brethren in the ALLIANCE. Moreover, no one appreciates, more fully than he, the fact that the record of our Quarter Century has in good measure been written by their noble, faithful and efficient lives. But the object of this memorial volume has not been to exploit the living, but to commemorate the dead. Indeed, the aim has been to make the history a record, not of human personalities, but of Divine Providences.

Second, no pains has been spared to make the Memorial chapter as complete as possible. In some instances, however, the facts could not be ascertained. On one mission field, for example, a personal search was instituted, but no records could be found to supply the needed information. Nevertheless, sincere regret is expressed for any gaps or mistakes in the work. For the gathering and arranging of much of the material of the Memorial chapter, the writer hereby acknowledges his indebtedness to the minute and painstaking researches of his wife.

Introduction.

I feel some natural hesitation in introducing a volume which in the nature of things so intimately and yet so unavoidably concerns my personal life and work. It would have been false modesty to have forbidden in a record of the past twenty-five years the references which so directly concern myself. At the same time I may be allowed to say that I have been kindly excused from any part whatever in writing or even contributing to this review. In looking over the proof with a view to preparing this introduction I have taken the liberty of correcting any inaccuracies which my better knowledge of the facts enabled me to appreciate. Otherwise the work is wholly due to the painstaking loyalty, and distinguished ability of my beloved brother, Doctor Pardington.

No one probably can realize so fully as myself the wonderful touch of God in the story of these twenty-five years. Indeed, the springs and sources of this work go back to a somewhat earlier period. I can well remember the nights I walked up and down the sandy beach at Old Orchard, Maine, in the summer of 1881, now thirty-three years ago, and asked God in some way to raise up a great missionary movement that would reach the neglected fields of the world, and utilize the neglected forces of the church at home as was not then being done. I little dreamed that I should have some little part in such a movement, but even then the vision was given of souls yet to be born like the stars of heaven and the sands upon that seashore. The movement has been wholly providential. Notwithstanding all its imperfections, the humble workers built better than they knew. Although the work is still but a beginning, yet we thank God for a consecrated army of more than a thousand men and women in our home and foreign fields, whose supreme watchword is the fulness of Jesus for His people and the evangelization of the world in the present generation.

The work has always looked to God alone for men and means, and in answer to be-

lieving prayer it is our privilege to thank
God for more than four millions of dollars
already expended in our work of evangelization. It would seem as if the time had
come when we are justified in appealing to
the larger constituency of our Christian
brethren in all the evangelical churches for
some expression of their fellowship and co-
operation in a movement which has surely
won the right to be accorded a place among
the Christian forces of to-day.

We trust that the story of these eventful
years, as told so simply and yet impressive-
ly by the gifted writer of this volume, will
so second and emphasize this appeal that
the work shall be strengthened by a wide
circle of new and helpful friends, and the
testimony of what God hath wrought will
encourage others in works of faith and labors of love.

The volume begins with a discriminating
survey of the religious conditions out of
which the Alliance movement crystallized
a generation ago, and then traces with
rapid but graphic touch the early history
of the movement and the beginning of the
local work in New York City with the

great circle of national and international conventions which gradually followed, leading at length to the incorporation of the two societies respectively for home and foreign work in 1889 and 1890. Then follows a statement of the fundamental principles and the specific testimony of the Christian Alliance, a testimony which has found expression in the well known phrase, "The Fourfold Gospel." Doctor Pardington points out the important place of this testimony as "present truth" and the need of this great and living message in all the churches to-day. His clear and comprehensive statement is of great value in establishing the true and permanent place of this providential movement and guarding it against misconstruction and prejudice.

It continues the story of the gradual shaping of the entire policy of the work culminating in 1897 in the consolidation of the two societies and the reorganization of the work under its present name as THE CHRISTIAN AND MISSIONARY ALLIANCE. The constitution and polity of the society are carefully outlined.

Perhaps the most interesting chapters are two that are devoted to the history of our missionary work and the sketching of its rapid expansion and present condition in nearly a score of great mission fields. The final chapter has a sacred interest to many as a brief memorial of more than one hundred consecrated lives that have joined our roll of honor during the past thirty years.

The work is fully illustrated with a number of cuts. The Society is deeply indebted to Doctor Pardington for this valuable contribution to the permanent literature of our work and the painstaking care with which he has saved from oblivion many records which in the coming years will be of increasing interest and value to the friends of the Alliance.

In revising the above introduction for a second edition of this work, it becomes our mournful duty to record the great loss which we have sustained in the recent death of our beloved brother, Dr. George P. Pardington. He was called to the presence of his Master after a few hours' illness on Sunday, March 28, 1915. His passing has left a blank that will not soon be filled and calls for a fuller memorial than these few lines permit.

The writer has known him since his boyhood, and vividly recalls his early healing, his college studies, and his intense ambition to acquire a liberal education that he might use it for the honor of his Master and especially for the Alliance work which he so dearly loved. After a brief ministry in the Methodist Episcopal Church, he joined the staff of the Missionary Institute in 1897, to which he has given the best that was in him during the past eighteen years. With a keener and larger vision than most of his brethren, he had grasped the special message of the Alliance and it was his delight to unfold it to his students as the very heart of the gospel. With a wide and accurate scholarship, a clear and brilliant mind, and above all with a fervor that won the sympathy and enthusiasm of his classes, he was an ideal teacher. His nature was most affectionate and lovable, and the simple words, "Our Friend" outlined on the floral piece given by the Academy students expressed their relations with him. God gave him a special vision for the Missionary Institute, and it was the supreme ambition of his life to have a leading part in working this out. It was said at the Memorial Service, "God permitted him in the last months of his life to enter into the full realization of his great ambition, and then in a moment the vision was crystallized, the picture was stereotyped, and like a sun, full-orbed and largest at its setting, he passed from our horizon to shine in other skies." He was the author of a volume which contains the very cream of his Institute teachings, "The Crisis of the Deeper Life." But the present volume will always remain his most precious memorial.

CHAPTER I

A STUDY IN ORIGINS

THE Christian and Missionary Alliance is not an isolated movement. It has spiritual kinships and historic origins.

THE SILVER THREAD OF TRUTH AND GRACE.

God has never left Himself without witnesses. Running through the Christian centuries is what may be called the silver thread of truth and grace. This is composed of companies of believers who have emphasized in their teaching and exemplified in their living the primitive truth and testimony of the New Testament. With this practically unbroken line of Apostolic piety and power the Christian and Missionary Alliance may claim close and vital spiritual kinship.

PROVIDENTIAL MOVEMENTS OF THE LAST CENTURY.

The last century witnessed the rise of five providential movements whose spirit and purpose fused and focused in the Christian and Missionary Alliance.

GOSPEL EVANGELISM.

There was first the evangelistic movement to give the Gospel to the non-church going masses. Beginning perhaps with the work of Charles G. Finney, this movement found its conspicuous representatives in Moody and Sankey and in Whittle and Bliss, through whose combined ministry of Gospel preaching and Gospel singing both Great Britain and America were stirred with a great awakening and swept with a revival flame. Sluggish Christians were aroused. Backsliders were reclaimed. Sinners were saved. Multitudes to-day in all walks of life date their conversion to God or full consecration to His service to this evangelistic movement of a generation or more ago.

HOLINESS.

Next in natural order came the Holiness movement. The generation that witnessed the beginning of the Christian and Missionary Alliance witnessed also the beginning in the hearts of believers in both Europe and America of a new spirit of faith and trust in God. Inspired in part by the wonderful work of George Muller there was a widespread hunger for the deepening of the spiritual life and for the enduement of the Holy Ghost for holy living and efficient serving. In England Dr. Horatius Bonar and Frances Ridley Havergal by voice and pen were active promoters of this movement. In this country Charles G. Finney stood quite as much for the entire sanctification of believers as for the full salvation of sinners. Indeed, in many ways Mr. Finney's wide ministry seems to have been a forerunner of the work of the Alliance. A little later Dr. and Mrs. Palmer, of New York, were prominent advocates of Scriptural holiness.

DIVINE HEALING.

The third movement of the last century was the revival of the Scriptural truth and practice of Divine Healing. On the continent the Home of Dorothea Trudel, in Minnedorf, Switzerland, and the Home of Pastor Blumhardt, in Mottlingen, in the Black Forest of Germany, were scenes of the marvelous restoration to health, by the healing power of Christ and in response to believing prayer, of multitudes suffering from organic diseases and incurable infirmities.

Similar instances of healing were witnessed under the ministry of Pastor Schwenk of Germany, Pastor Stockmeyer of Hauptweil, Switzerland, and Dr. W. E. Boardman and Mrs. M. Baxter at Bethshan, London. In this country, when the Alliance was organized, Dr. Charles Cullis, in his Faith Work, in Boston, Carrie F. Judd (now Carrie Judd Montgomery), in her Faith Rest in Buffalo, and "Father" Allen, of New England, besides Mrs. Mix and others, were being wonderfully used of God in the complete healing of countless persons afflicted with sicknesses and infirmities beyond the reach of medical or surgical aid.

FOREIGN MISSIONS.

The supreme movement of the last century was the great missionary awakening. Receiving its impulse and inspiration from the spirit and labors of William Carey, the holy zeal and consecrated enthusiasm of the little band of students in Williamstown, Massachusetts, who started "the haystack prayer meeting," aroused the evangelical churches of America to a new and deepened sense of their obligation to give the Gospel to the heathen world. Since that wonderful year of 1810 there has been a steadily rising tide of missionary praying, missionary giving, and missionary going.

THE LORD'S RETURN.

The crowning spiritual movement of the last century was the renewed interest in the personal, pre-millennial, and imminent return of the Lord Jesus. In Europe the leaders in advocacy of Scriptural Holiness and Divine Healing have stood also for the most part for the truth of the Lord's return. In this country Dr. James H. Brooks, of Saint Louis, and Dr. A. J. Gorden, of Boston, were in the forefront of this precious movement which has refreshed and blessed the whole body of Christ.

The fact that the Christian and Missionary Alliance in its teaching and testimony embodies and exemplifies the spirit and purpose of these five spiritual movements of the nineteenth century is a witness at once to its providential inception, its Scriptural foundation, and its complete adaptation to meet and satisfy the varied needs of spirit, soul, and body.

SKETCH OF THE EARLIER LIFE OF THE REV. A. B. SIMPSON.

From the beginning the Christian and Missionary Alliance to a remarkable degree has been an impersonal movement; that is, it is a movement not so much of human leadership as of Divine truths and spiritual forces. At the same time, its origin cannot be understood apart from the Lord's dealings with its founder and president.

EARLY YEARS.

Albert B. Simpson was born December 15, 1844, at Bay View, Prince Edward's Island, Dominion of Canada. He came of Scotch Presbyterian ancestry, his parents being James and Jane (Clark) Simpson. When Albert was about three years old the family removed to Kent County, Western Ontario, the boy receiving his early education at the Chatham High School. With the ministry in view young Simpson and his brother, the late Rev. W. H. Simpson, entered Knox College, Toronto, the former being graduated in 1865 and the latter in 1866. It is of curious interest to note that during his seminary days Mr. Simpson wrote a prize paper in favor of infant baptism.

HAMILTON, ONTARIO.

In 1865 Mr. Simpson was married to Miss Margaret L. Henry, of Toronto. The same year he was ordained to the Christian ministry and installed as pastor of Knox Church, the second strongest United Presbyterian church in Canada. Here he remained for about eight years, the membership of the church growing from three hundred to seven hundred.

LOUISVILLE, KENTUCKY.

Owing to the ill effects of the rigorous climate of Western Ontario upon his health, late in the fall of 1873 Mr. Simpson accepted a unanimous invitation to the Chestnut Street Presbyterian Church, in Louisville, Kentucky, beginning his pastorate early in 1874.

There were in Louisville northern and southern churches of the same evangelical denominations. Through the instrumentality of Mr. Simpson the pastors of these different churches for the first time since the civil war united in 1875 in inviting Whittle and Bliss to hold a Gospel campaign in the city. As a result Louisville was visited with a great religious awakening. Mr. Simpson himself was deeply stirred by these meetings and the Lord gave him an intense desire to preach the Gospel to the non-church going masses. Failing to obtain the support of other pastors, Mr. Simpson and his church alone undertook to carry on an evangelistic campaign among the unsaved. For two winters every Sunday night he preached, first in Public Library Hall and then in Macauley's Theater. Indeed, at this time Mr. Simpson was convinced that the Lord wanted him to lead the life of an evangelist.

During the Whittle and Bliss campaign Mr. Simpson and his people realized the need of a building more centrally located and more generally adapted to reach the non-church going middle classes. The outcome of much praying and planning was the Broadway Tabernacle (afterwards the Warren Memorial Church), one of the most beautiful and commodious structures for religious purposes in the country.

But in the midst of his arduous labors and

from the long strain of overwork Mr. Simpson's health broke. While resting he experienced a touch of the Lord's life for his body. He also gave serious thought to issuing an illustrated missionary magazine.

In 1880 Mr. Simpson accepted a unanimous call to the Thirteenth Street Presbyterian Church, New York City. By invitation of the pastor, the Rev. Dr. Burchard, he had previously preached there when a delegate to the Evangelical Alliance. His chief reason in removing from Louisville to New York was the publication of the missionary journal which was on his heart. During the two years he was pastor of the Thirteenth Street Church Mr. Simpson passed through the great spiritual and ministerial crisis of his life.

ILLUSTRATED MISSIONARY MAGAZINE.

Soon after going to New York Mr. Simpson began the publication of his projected illustrated missionary magazine, "The Gospel in All Lands," which was transferred in 1881, to Rev. Eugene Smith and afterwards issued by the missionary society of the Methodist Episcopal Church.

NON-CHURCH GOING MASSES.

The vast throngs of non-church goers in New York City were laid heavily on Mr. Simpson's heart. He desired to preach the Gospel to them on the street or in public halls, as he had done in Louisville. He made a personal canvass of the ninth ward, visiting every home. In his praying and planning he conceived a church without pew rents and for all classes and conditions of men, something like Newman Hall's church, or Spurgeon's Tabernacle, in London, England.

BAPTISM BY IMMERSION.

In 1881 Mr. Simpson began to be troubled in his mind about the question of baptism. He became deeply impressed, and in his closet laid the whole matter before the Lord with a prayer for light. He was led carefully and prayerfully to compare all the Scripture passages on the subject, reaching the conclusion that he should be baptized by immersion. Accordingly, in obedience to his conscience and before he met the Presbytery of his church he was quietly baptized in the manner he believed to be taught in the Word of God. In a personal statement to his people soon afterwards **Mr. Simpson** said that he regarded baptism as a matter of individual conscience, that he had no wish to argue or even agitate the matter, and that he was not free to unite with another denomination which made baptism by immersion a term of communion.

PHYSICAL HEALING.

In 1881 the Lord healed Mr. Simpson of serious heart trouble. It happened on this wise. He spent part of his vacation that summer at Saratoga Springs. He was broken in health and discouraged in spirit. Wandering along the street he approached the Park where a band of Jubilee Singers were singing. Their song deeply impressed his mind and strangely warmed his heart:

"Nothing is too hard for Jesus,
No man can work like Him."

A few months later at Old Orchard, Me., he took the Lord definitely as his healer.

Through this simple and quaint melody the Holy Spirit spoke to Mr. Simpson. At the time of his healing Mr. Simpson tells us he made a threefold covenant with the Lord: First, he planted his feet firmly on the truth of Divine healing, as revealed in the Scriptures. Second, he definitely appropriated the Lord's life for his body, indeed, taking the Lord not only for every need of mind and body, but also for every pressure and emergency of his work. And third, he received this truth and this life from the hands of the Lord in solemn trust and sacred ministry for others.

WITHDRAWAL FROM CHURCH AND MINISTRY.

Late in 1881 Mr. Simpson resigned the pastorate of his church and withdrew his membership from the New York presbytery. In taking this step he was influenced by the call of God to give the Gospel to the non-church going classes.

Reluctantly the Thirteenth Street Church consented to allow its pastor to retire, for their mutual relations were cordial and affectionate. Indeed, in leaving Mr. Simpson earnestly urged his people not to follow him, but to remain and work together for the best interests of the church. Reluctantly moreover the New York presbytery consented to Mr. Simpson's withdrawal of membership, for his relations with that body were harmonious and fraternal.

THE GOSPEL TABERNACLE, NEW YORK CITY.

The Gospel Tabernacle, of New York City, has been the fostering mother of the Christian and Missionary Alliance. Indeed, just as the Tabernacle is the expression in concrete form of the spiritual convictions and providential experiences of its pastor, so the Alliance is a projection, on a world-wide scale, of the Tabernacle.

ORGANIZATION.

In November, 1881, Mr. Simpson resigned the pastorate of the Thirteenth Street Church. Soon after he began to hold Gospel services in Caledonian Hall, a dance hall on Thirteenth Street, opposite Jackson Square. "At the first meeting Mr. Simpson invited all who desired to co-operate in the new evangelical work to meet for prayer during the week. He also stated that simply depending on God for the pecuniary support of himself and family, and the means necessary to carry on the work, he should not apply to any human channel for aid, and should only accept the voluntary offerings of those who wished to assist by their contributions. From the very beginning the presence of the Holy Ghost was graciously manifested in constant conversions." February 10, 1882, the little flock met at Mr. Simpson's residence and formally organized in the name of the Lord Jesus a church consisting of thirty-five members. The following Sunday they with a number of other persons sat down for the first time together at the Lord's Table. The same year the society was incorporated as an independent church, "organized for the especial purpose of Gospel work, particularly among the neglected classes, both at home and abroad."

CHANGES OF LOCATION.

For seven years, like the children of Israel in the wilderness, the little flock pitched its tent wherever the providence of God directed. The work of the church has been carried on in the following places: Caledonian Hall, Academy of Music, Steinway Hall, Abbey's Park Theater, Grand Opera Hall, Madison Square Garden, Gospel tents in Twenty-third Street, Thirtieth Street, and Fifty-fifth Street, Twenty-third Street Theater, Madison Avenue Tabernacle, Standard Hall, and the Gospel Tabernacle, Eighth Avenue, near Forty-fourth Street.

These many removals and the strange vicissitudes would have destroyed the work, unless it had been of God. Three of the
changes call for special note.

Centrally located on West Twenty-third
Street, near Sixth Avenue, was an old ar-
mory building, the two lower floors being
used as a livery stable: Twice Mr. Simpson tried to secure this building. The second time he found that it had been leased
for five years by Salmi Morse for the production of the blasphemous "Passion Play."
A member of the church, a woman, prayed:
"O Lord Jesus, make the carpenters fit up
that place for us. Make the Passion people
decorate and furnish it for us. We cannot
afford to pay $15,000 to do it ourselves." At
the re-dedication of the Twenty-third Street
Theater as a church in 1884, Mr. Simpson
said: "God did put His hand upon it, and
He did stop the public production of that
play. After spending $70,000 in remodelling
the building the project broke down and
the company gave up the lease. They offered to sell us their improvements for
$5,000. We prayed over it, but God stopped
us from going too fast. The building was

finally put into the market and sold at auction, and the gentleman bought who we prayed would buy it. The result is that we have been enabled to come in here without paying a penny for the improvements."

In 1886 Mr. Simpson and his people went to the Madison Avenue Congregational Church, corner of Forty-fifth Street. This was a huge iron structure built for Dr. George H. Hepworth and afterwards occupied by Dr. (later Bishop) John P. Newman, of the Methodist Episcopal Church. This edifice was occupied for about three years, and then sold because the neighborhood was unsuited to carry on evangelistic work among the unsaved.

In 1889 the present Gospel Tabernacle was erected. The location and structure are well adapted to the varied work of the church. The building is situated on the east side of Eighth Avenue, near the corner of 44th Street. The front of the structure is occupied by stores, while above them rises the Missionary Home and the official rooms of the Christian and Missionary Alliance. Immediately in the rear of the stores stands the Tabernacle with its two chapels. It is semi-circular, and seated to accommodate about 1,000 persons.

DEPARTMENTS OF THE WORK AND AUXILIARY AGENCIES.

From the first the work of the Tabernacle was not designed as a mission to the lowest and vicious classes, but as a self-supporting work among the middle classes who have no home. But as the providence of God directed, a network of related departments and auxiliary agencies to meet the varied needs of all classes and conditions of men came into existence. A few of these may be mentioned:

Berachah Home for rest and healing began its work in 1883 at 331 West Thirty-fourth Street.

Berachah Mission at Tenth Avenue and Thirty-second Street, in what was known as "Hell's Kitchen," was opened in 1885. There were Gospel Missions also on Eleventh Avenue and on South Street.

One of the first institutions was a home for fallen women in West Twenty-seventh Street, where many of the wretched women who crowded that part of the city were saved.

The New York Missionary Training College for evangelists, missionaries, and Christian workers was started in 1883, the early classes being held on the stage of the old Twenty-third Street theater. The first commencement was held in the spring of 1884, and in November of the same year the first missionary party of seven sailed for the Congo.

In 1888 Berachah Orphanage was opened for the purpose of providing a home for those left destitute of parental care.

One of the earliest organizations was the German branch of the Tabernacle.

Soon after discontinuing "The Gospel in All Lands," Mr. Simpson began the publication of "The Word, Work, and World," an illustrated magazine. This journal completed its ninth volume in 1887.

SPIRITUAL AND PERMANENT RESULTS.

From the beginning the Tabernacle has been a veritable beehive of Christian activity. The inworking and outworking of spiritual forces cannot be computed in numbers nor expressed in rhetoric. But a few striking facts may be noted:

MISSIONARY INSTITUTE. NYACK. N. Y.

The accepted motto of the Tabernacle from the start seems to have been a work for every one and every one at work. In addition to the associated departments and auxiliary agencies of the church, the consecrated energies of the members, particularly of the young people, have been directed to holding open air meetings, services in jails, hospitals, on shipboard in the harbor, and in many other places, wherever in fact doors of opportunity are opened by the providence of God.

Multitudes were converted at the tent meetings in the early years, while at the regular services of the Tabernacle souls are constantly being saved. The message of the Tabernacle pulpit has always been the fulness of Jesus for body, soul, and spirit, and the baptism of the Holy Ghost for effective Christian service at home and abroad.

First in the early tent meetings and at the pastor's residence and later in Berachah Home hundreds were healed of hopeless diseases and incurable infirmities. Sufferers from consumption, tumor, cancer, and other fatal maladies were completely and in many instances instantly healed by simple faith through the power of the living Christ. Friday afternoon at three o'clock a Divine Healing meeting is held in the Tabernacle. In Greater New York and indeed throughout the entire country the "Friday Meeting" is as well known as the famous Fulton Street Noon Prayer Meeting. It has from the beginning witnessed the healing of hundreds of persons suffering from chronic diseases and confirmed invalidism. Out of the work of healing in the early years grew a volume of remarkable testimonies, called "The Cloud of Witnesses."

Naturally many Christians from other churches have been drawn to the Tabernacle. Such have always been welcomed, and many have been among the staunchest friends and supporters of the work. But from the outset it has been the aim of the Tabernacle to create its own membership and establish its own constituency. The primary purpose has been to save souls. Then the new converts have been led on into the fulness of Jesus, taught to become soul-winners, and, where they have gifts and graces, trained for evangelistic work or missionary service. This is the Apostolic method. It has moreover a great practical advantage. New converts do not have to be delivered from the vain traditions of their fathers. They have no doctrinal prepossessions or church prejudices to overcome. They are easily led into the deeper truths of sanctification, Divine Healing, and the Lord's return. Moreover, they take to Christian work as a matter of course, and when truly called and anointed of God make successful evangelists and efficient missionaries.

CHAPTER II

THE MARCH OF EVENTS

1914 and 1915 mark the quarter-centennial of the legal incorporation of the International Missionary Alliance and the Christian Alliance, the two societies which afterwards became the Christian and Missionary Alliance.

Twenty-five wonderful years! Truly, their record is written in heaven, and their influence has gone out to the ends of the earth. What pen can fully compass or adequately portray the story of simple faith and mighty achievement, of faithful labor and heroic sacrifice. Out of the annals of the past there are five forward movements and historic events which must have special treatment and permanent record.

INITIAL SPIRITUAL IMPULSE.

It was inevitable that the varied work of the Gospel Tabernacle in New York City should become known far and wide. Indeed, countless letters of inquiry and re-

quests for prayer were received from all
parts of the country, showing that God was
creating in the hearts of His people a deep
hunger for spiritual truth and physical help
and an intense desire to meet in some practical way the obligation to give the Gospel
to the heathen world. To reach as far as
possible this wider constituency it was decided to hold a summer assembly. Thus it
came about that in in 1886 the first Old Orchard Convention was held.

A mile back from the seacoast at Old Orchard, Maine, the configuration of the land
has formed a vast amphitheater, capacious
enough to seat several thousand persons.
Here there was a famous camp ground,
where for years the National Holiness Association and other organizations held their
annual assemblies. This indeed was the
spot where Mr. Simpson had found the Lord
as his Healer. Here Dr. Cullis, of Boston,
had for many years held a larger summer
meeting. But he had abandoned it for a
new camp ground at Intervale, N. H. In
1885 a deputation from Old Orchard consisting of Messrs. Luce and Chase visited
New York and invited Mr. Simpson to take

up that meeting at Old Orchard, and in the following summer he did so. Here in this beautiful and hallowed pine grove a large company of the Lord's people met in convocation, and for several days their hearts were stirred by teaching on the deeper Christian life and by the presentation of the needs of the heathen fields. It was indeed a mount of vision and inspiration. Both the leader and the people were moved by mighty spiritual forces, first in the direction of a bond of union and fellowship which would unite Christians of all evangelical churches who believed in the fulness of Jesus and in the baptism of the Holy Ghost, and second in the direction of a simple organization which would convert missionary consecration and enthusiasm into practical measures for the speedy evangelization of the world.

The following summer, 1887, at the second Old Orchard Convention, the spiritual forces and missionary impulses, which had so mightily stirred the assembly a year before, found concrete expression in the organization of the Christian Alliance and the Evangelical Missionary Alliance.

OLD ORCHARD CAMP GROUND.

TABERNACLE. OLD ORCHARD CAMP GROUND.

LEGAL INCORPORATION.

From a legal standpoint, 1889 marks the beginning of Alliance history. On the second day of November of that year the International Missionary Alliance (formerly the Evangelical Missionary Alliance) was incorporated. Moreover, on the nineteenth day of September, 1890, the Christian Alliance was incorporated. Both societies were incorporated according to the laws of the state of New York.

CHRISTIAN ALLIANCE.

In the certificate of incorporation it is stated "That the particular business and object of such Society are the wide diffusion of the Gospel in its fulness, the promotion of a deeper and higher Christian life, and the work of evangelization especially among the neglected classes by highway missions and other practical methods."

INTERNATIONAL MISSIONARY ALLIANCE.

In the certificate of incorporation it is stated "That the particular business and objects of such Society is the preaching of the Gospel in North America and in foreign lands, the promotion of evangelical domestic and foreign missions, and the training of missionaries for such domestic and foreign missionary work."

CONSOLIDATION OF THE TWO SOCIETIES.

For seven or eight years the Christian Alliance and the International Missionary Alliance had a separate existence, doing their work along parallel lines. During this time there was a growing conviction that amalgamation would be to the mutual advantage of both societies. In this annual report in the spring of 1896 the president said:

"The proposed amalgamation, it is believed, will greatly simplify the work of both Societies, reduce expenses, and promote the efficiency of both.

"The real objects of the two Societies are largely identical. The one is really the complement of the other. The Christian Alliance is the sustaining constituency of the Missionary Alliance, and the Missionary Alliance is the outlet of the Christian Alliance. Hand in hand they have walked and worked together for the witness of Jesus and the evangelization of the neglected at home and abroad, and now God seems to proclaim the banns of a heavenly marriage, and to say, 'What God hath joined together let not man put asunder.'"

THE CHRISTIAN AND MISSIONARY ALLIANCE.

On the second day of April, 1897, an agreement for consolidation was effected between the Christian Alliance and the International Missionary Alliance, the two Societies being incorporated under the laws of the state of New York as THE CHRISTIAN AND MISSIONARY ALLIANCE.

In the agreement for consolidation it is stated "That the objects of the New Corporation shall be to bear witness to the Christian truths, especially those relating to the deeper Christian life, and at home and abroad to preach the Gospel; to evangelize the neglected classes, to establish and maintain mission stations, to prosecute mission work, and to erect and to assist in erecting such buildings as may be necessary for such purposes."

It is also stated "That the date of the first annual corporate meeting of the New Corporation shall be Good Friday in the year 1898.

In his first annual report of the new organization, in the spring of 1898, the president said:

"This year will be memorable as the first year of the consolidation of the Christian and Missionary Alliance. The union which was formally consummated a year ago has been getting into practical operation during the past twelve months. * * *

"The year has been one of settling and stablishing and your president and board of managers are able to report that the work is now resting on a stronger and broader foundation than ever before. * * *

"The hearts of our people and especially of our workers have been confirmed in a deep sense of our divine and heavenly calling as an Alliance, and we are going forth into another year with a profounder conviction of our sacred mission and a deeper unity and fellowship in this great trust than ever before."

Nyack Heights.

In 1897 Nyack Heights was founded as a new center of Alliance work. Nyack Heights is in the pretty village of South Nyack, Rockland County, New York, situated on the right bank of the Hudson River and about twenty-eight miles from Jersey City.

The Nyack Heights Land and Improvement Company, which was incorporated in 1897, purchased a tract of several acres on Old South Mountain with a view to its development for residential purposes and institutional work.

The outlook from the mountain side is unsurpassed. A panorama of the Hudson River valley for twenty miles lies spread out at one's feet. The entire region is famed in history and steeped in legend. Across the river are Ossining, Tarrytown, and Irvington, the heights beyond and above studded with costly and beautiful residences. Within sight are Lyndhurst, the summer home of Helen Gould Shepard, "Sunnyside," the old home of Washington Irving, Sleepy Hollow, made famous by Irving in "The Legend of Sleepy Hollow," and on Pocantico Hills the country estate of John D. Rockefeller. On the north at one's feet nestles the staid and quaint town of Nyack, guarded like a sentinel by Hook Mountain. On the south opens the broad expanse of the Tappan-Zee, and beyond is the famous ridge of the Palisades along which the majestic Hudson sweeps onward to the sea. The River Road from Sparkill past the picturesque villages of Piermont and Grand View and on through Nyack up to Hook Mountain is a fascinating driveway of seven miles amid river, town and valley scenery. A state road direct from New York City to Harriman Park in the Catskill Mountains is under construction. This broad boulevard will sweep past the foot of Old South Mountain.

Nyack Heights is the educational center of the Alliance. On the lower terrace near Hillside Avenue is the Wilson Memorial Academy with its adjoining gymnasium. This is a plain but attractive structure capable of accommodating about one hundred boarding students. A little above is pretty Hillside Chapel. Crowning the mountain side at an elevation of about four hundred feet is the familiar and substantial Missionary Institute, a building of noble and graceful proportions with accommodations for fully two hundred boarding students. To the north on the site of the old Tabernacle an Administrative and Recitation Hall has recently been erected. This simple and

commodious building is of an impressive
style of architecture and presents a striking
and beautiful appearance. Besides administrative offices it contains an auditorium capable with adjoining rooms of seating about
eight hundred persons. There are nearly a
score of study, library, and class rooms.
The building is steam heated, electrically
lighted, and when fully equipped will be ad-
mirably adapted in every way to the varied
and important work of the Nyack Schools.

Midway up the mountain side is Berachah
Home, occupying the commodious and com-
fortable residence formerly owned by Ross
Taylor. The ample grounds and beautiful
surroundings invest the place with a quiet
and restful charm.

Nyack Heights has become a residential
center for many official workers and for a
growing number of Alliance families. More
than a dozen pretty cottages and beautiful
residences already dot the Hillside. The
pure water, the fresh mountain air, the reasonable price of land, the charming scenery,
the quiet and comforts of country life, ready
access to New York City, and the un-
equalled educational advantages are among

the chief compelling attractions of Nyack Heights.

PRAYER CONFERENCE ON TRUTH AND TESTIMONY.

In May, 1906, an important prayer conference on truth and testimony was held in connection with the Annual Council, at Nyack. In the official literature of course the truths for which the Alliance stands have always been unfolded with unmistakable clearness and unvarying emphasis. But for a considerable time, on the part of some speakers at conventions, there had been a noticeable lack of agreement in the presentation of the doctrinal positions and distinctive teachings of the movement. Because of this fact, much confusion existed in the minds of many people as to exactly what the Alliance stands for and exactly what it does not stand for. Consequently, it was deemed wise to summon the leading teachers and official workers for season of prayer and conference as to the public presentation of Alliance truth and testimony. Various brethren read carefully prepared papers on the Fourfold Gospel, which were followed by open and informal discussion. The results of these days of prayer and conference were most gratifying. The atmosphere was cleared of confusion. Doctrinal bearings were freshly taken and newly emphasized. Since then, indeed, there has been a marked unity and clearness of Alliance teaching which has been felt for good in all parts of the work.

New Constitution.

In 1912, the Annual Council at Boone, Iowa, adopted a new constitution. By the natural process of extension and development many features of the polity of the old constitution had been outgrown. In his annual report at Boone the president said:

"The changes proposed do not involve any modification of our testimony or spiritual life, but only concern the administration of the work. The new constitution aims specially at giving a larger responsibility and authority to the general Council, a more independent and automatic self-government to the different localities, and a more systematic administration of the entire executive work. It contemplates such a unification of our entire educational system as will secure a better grading of all the students, a more perfect and complete provision for the higher educational training on the part of all who are qualified to receive it, greater economy of forces and resources by system and co-operation, and a more general development of local schools in various sections of the country."

CHAPTER III

THE FULNESS OF JESUS

THE Gospel message of the Christian and Missionary Alliance is the Fulness of Jesus through the indwelling and power of the Holy Ghost to meet and satisfy every need of spirit, soul, and body.

EVANGELICAL BASIS.

The doctrinal basis of the Alliance is strictly evangelical. In common with orthodox Protestantism it unhesitatingly accepts and unequivocally teaches the fundamental truths of the Holy Scriptures. Aside from the Word of God it has no formal creed.

DECLARATION OF FAITH AND PRINCIPLES.

At the same time, prospective missionaries and applicants for membership must be prepared to sign the following simple declaration of faith and principles:

"I believe in God the Father, Son, and Holy Ghost, in the verbal inspiration of the

Holy Scriptures as originally given, in the vicarious atonement of the Lord Jesus Christ, in the eternal salvation of all who believe in Him and in the everlasting punishment of all who reject Him. I believe in the Lord Jesus Christ as my Saviour, Sanctifier, Healer, and Coming Lord. I am in full sympathy with the principles and objects of the Christian and Missionary Alliance, and shall earnestly endeavor to promote them in every proper way."

PARAMOUNT CALLING.

But while evangelical in doctrinal basis, the Alliance has a paramount calling and a distinctive testimony:

"Pre-eminently we are witnesses for Christ. We are glad to testify to Him before we speak of His blessings or gifts to men. It is Christ as a Person, as a living reality, as the supreme fact of history and Life, Jesus Himself, who is the theme of our testimony. Soon He is to appear in the vivid and glorious revelation of His personal majesty, filling all earth and heaven. But meanwhile He is projecting His personality upon the age, upon the thought and heart of His people, and upon our individual lives, and He wants us to know Him, to represent Him, and to reveal Him to men. Above everything else this is a Christ movement. If we are saved it is Christ who saves us. If we are sanctified it is Christ who is made unto us sanctification. If we are healed it is because His life is in us. And the hope of the future is not the glory He is to reveal, but the return of the King Himself, our Beloved and our Friend."

In short, to give Christ to the sinner; to make Christ real to the believer; to present Christ in His fulness through the power of the indwelling Holy Ghost as the complete satisfaction of every need of spirit, mind, and body; to give Christ and the riches of His grace to the heathen world,—this is our special calling and distinctive testimony. In a word, the mission and message of the Christian and Missionary Alliance is to proclaim neglected Scripture truth and to prosecute neglected Christian work both at home and abroad:—"to give the whole Gospel to the whole world."

THE FOURFOLD GOSPEL.

Once when Dr. Henry Wilson was in

Canada a woman exultantly said to him, "I know what the 'fourfold Gospel' means. It means the four Gospels of Matthew, Mark, Luke, and John."

This of course is not the sense in which the words are used. Nor is the phrase a mathematical attempt to compass the benefits of the Gospel. The Gospel of Christ is manifold and its blessings are infinite. "The Fourfold Gospel" is simply a striking watchword, which expresses the paramount calling and distinctive testimony of the Alliance. Thus it stands for the cardinal doctrinal truths of the movement.

CHRIST OUR SAVIOUR
CHRIST OUR SANCTIFIER
CHRIST OUR HEALER
CHRIST OUR COMING LORD

CHRIST OUR SAVIOUR.

The primary message of the Alliance is the primary message of the Gospel, and that is to the sinner. We believe that man is a sinner, that the sinner is lost, and that there is no other name given under heaven and among men whereby a lost sinner can be saved but the Name of Jesus. Sin, it is held, is not an accident or an imperfection, not an amiable weakness or an infirmity, not misfortune or heredity. Sin is a terrible reality, a wilful transgression of Divine law, a wicked enmity of mind and alienation of heart towards God. Sin has outraged the holiness of God, whose justice demands satisfaction. The sinner is a rebel, under Divine condemnation and exposed to the just punishment of everlasting death.

But while believing in the terrible reality of sin, the Alliance believes also in the glorious reality of the atonement for sin. We believe that God loves sinners, and gave His only-begotten to die for them. We believe that Christ was "delivered for our offences and raised again for our justification." We believe in the cross of Calvary and in the power of the blood to save men.

The Alliance believes, furthermore, that God's offer of salvation is as wide as humanity and that His pardon and forgiveness are for all who truly repent of their sins and fully accept Christ as their Saviour. Indeed, we believe that "the moment a sinner accepts this Gospel, his sins are forgiven, his soul is regenerated, he becomes a child of God, and an heir of glory, and has 'access by faith into the grace wherein we stand,' and all the rights and privileges of the family of God."

Most emphatically, the Alliance has no kinship or sympathy with modern methods of salvation by character or culture. Neither education nor reformation can change either the Ethiopian skin or the leopard spots of the sinner. Most emphatically, we do believe in spiritual regeneration, in the birth from above, in the new creature in Christ Jesus. Salvation gives life to the dead, the "dead in trespasses and sins"; and the sinner who accepts the Gospel of grace in Christ Jesus is thereby delivered from the power of darkness and translated into the kingdom of God.

Thus the primary message of the Alliance is Christ our Saviour. Our first business for the King is the salvation of sinners. To win souls is our fundamental ministry. Indeed, to lie in wait for men like the Master Himself and with a wisdom and skill that are born from above to catch them in the net of the Gospel is the highest calling of the surrendered and consecrated Christian.

Every Alliance Branch, like every evangelical church, should be first and foremost a life-saving station for the salvation of souls. No Alliance leader or worker at home or abroad, and no pastor or evangelist is truly equipped for the Lord's vineyard unless like the Master Himself, when he sees the multitude he is "moved with compassion on them, because they faint and are as sheep having no shepherd." Is it not unreasonable and inconsistent to be concerned for the salvation of heathen abroad and not be burdened for the conversion of sinners at home? Let no Alliance leader or member, no pastor or church member rest satisfied till he has experienced a deep and abiding spiritual birth travail. From every devout heart may the fervent prayer ascend, "Lord, give me a passion for souls."

CHRIST OUR SANCTIFIER.

The deeper message of the Alliance is the deeper message of the Gospel, and that is the entire sanctification of the spirit, soul, and body of the child of God. But it is our clear and unmistakable teaching that the life of entire sanctification is entered by a definite experience, a definite experience which has been happily expressed "the crisis of the deeper life." This crisis is marked, it is held, by the reception of the person of the Holy Ghost who brings Christ to indwell and possess the heart and life. And the only condition of receiving the Holy Spirit is a step of complete surrender and an act of appropriating faith. After this crisis experience sanctification is, we believe, gradual in the sense of the development and full maturity of the life "hid with Christ in God." Mighty is the transformation wrought by Divine regeneration, but this after all is only the initial experience of the Christian life. We get a good deal indeed, but we do not get everything, in regeneration. Nor does regeneration give the germ, the embryo, out of which by the process of growth and development every later phase of Christian experience is evolved. Regeneration imparts a new Divine life, which takes away the love of sin; but sanctification brings a new Divine Person, who delivers from the power of sin. Regeneration alone means constant struggle and certain defeat in warfare against the world, the flesh and the devil. But rest from struggle and victory in conflict are assured through the incoming of the Holy Spirit and the indwelling of the risen Christ. But this involves a new experience, a second definite work of grace,—a crisis as radical and revolutionary as the crisis of regeneration. In regeneration we pass out of death into life; but in sanctification we pass out of the self-life into the Christ life. In regeneration we receive a new spirit; but in sanctification we receive the Holy Spirit. After the experience of regeneration the Holy Spirit is with us; but through the experience of sanctification He is in us. In regeneration the Holy Spirit builds the temple; but in sanctification He moves in and occupies it.

From the beginning it has been the spirit and aim of the Alliance not so much to preach doctrines as to preach Christ. It has been the desire to avoid the controversial side of disputed questions and to present "the fulness of Jesus for Christian life and service." Take, for example, the suggestive and attractive watchword: "Christ our Sanctifier." This simple phrase expresses at once the highest fact and the profoundest philosophy of holiness. On this supremely important theme it is our mission and our message to present the living Lord, who is "made unto us sanctification." So far as possible we leave the plane of abstract theory and rise to the sublime but practical truth of the indwelling Christ. We do not, therefore, emphasize inner states and subjective experiences so much as we emphasize the Lord. We would not minimize the blessing, but we would magnify the Blesser. We do not like to talk about "it," but we love to talk about "Him."

But while emphasizing the person of Christ as the sanctifier of His people, the Alliance has always clearly and unmistakably stood for a "real genuine experience of righteousness of heart and life." Holiness is not a garment to conceal unrighteousness. It is not a veneering to hide a life spiritually untransformed. Sanctification, we insist, means renewed character and righteous conduct. It involves a radical revolution in personality. There is a deep and abiding transformation in the temper of the mind, in the disposition of the heart and in the bent of the will. But the blessing of a

ALLIANCE CHAPEL. PHILIPPINES.

clean heart is inseparable from the posses-
sion of the clean heart by the Holy Spirit.
Without His constant presence and full pos-
session the cleansing of the heart would not
be permanent. Sanctification is not ours
apart from the person of Christ. We are
holy only as we are in living union with the
Holy One. When we get Him, we get everything in Him. Thus our watchword for a
holy life and a fruitful ministry is:

"Everything in Jesus and Jesus everything."

CHRIST OUR HEALER.

The third vital message of the Alliance is
the gospel of physical healing. Yet while
the truth of Divine Healing is made of great
importance, it is held in strict subordination
to the pre-eminent truths of salvation and
holiness. The Alliance believes that sickness is the result of sin, in the sense that if
there had been no sin there would be no
sickness. But the Alliance also believes
that the benefits of the atonement are as
wide as the results of sin. The sure foundation of Divine Healing we find in the
promises of God, in the redemptive work of
Christ, and in the quickening power of the
Holy Spirit.

Most emphaticaly, the Christian and Missionary Alliance has nothing whatever in common with modern schools or methods of psychical healing, such as Christian Science, the Emmanuel movement, magnetic or spiritualistic healing, mind cure, or even faith cure. The Scriptural truth of Divine Healing is simply that, in answer to believing prayer, God honors His word and for the sake of Jesus stretches forth His mighty hand and recovers from their sicknesses and heals of their diseases those of His suffering children who live in obedience to His holy will. Sometimes indeed in His sovereign grace the Lord vouchsafes to heal even the sinning and the disobedient who thereby are saved and consecrate their lives wholly to Him.

During the past twenty-five years, in answer to the prayer of faith, literally thousands of persons have been raised from beds of sickness or healed of incurable infirmities by the direct power of God. It is well within the truth to say that of the many Christians from evangelical churches who have become members of the Alliance perhaps the majority have come into the move-

ment through a definite experience of
physical healing. Most of our missionaries
on the foreign field and our leaders and
workers at home have been healed of serious
and in many instances of incurable diseases.
Indeed, there is scarcely an Alliance member throughout the world who does not
know Christ as the Great Physician.

But the glorious truth of "Christ our
Healer" includes more than physical healing. It means the quickening and strengthening of our bodies by contact through the
Holy Spirit with our risen and triumphant
Lord. Whatever the explanation, it is a
fact that of those who take Christ as their
Healer some are not healed of their diseases
or delivered from their infirmities in the
sense that the diseases wholly disappear or
the infirmities are entirely removed. They
could not get a doctor's certificate of good
health nor, because of physical unsoundness,
could they take out a life insurance policy.
Yet such persons daily experience a supernatural quickening of their bodies which
gives them freshness and strength and in
some instances extraordinary physical endurance. Indeed, they seem to have some-

thing more than Divine Healing; they have
Divine life. Theirs indeed is a paradoxical
experience. Instead of being bedridden or
helpless invalids they keep going in the
strength of Jesus, not only carrying their
own burdens but stretching out a helping
hand to others. Surely it is one thing to
sink down under the power of disease or the
weight of infirmity; but it is quite another
thing to rise above the power of disease and
the weight of infirmity and in the strength
of the ascended and glorified Christ not only
have a victorious spirit but bear fruit, yea,
the "much fruit" that shall abide the day of
His coming. An experience like this is apostolic. With Paul its possessors can truly
say:

"But we had the sentence of death in ourselves, that we should not trust in ourselves, but in God which raiseth the dead:

"Who delivered us from so great a death,
and doth deliver: in whom we trust that He
will yet deliver us" (2 Cor. i: 9, 10).

And again:

"Always bearing about in the body the
dying of the Lord Jesus, that the life also of
Jesus might be made manifest in our body.

"For we which live are always delivered unto death for Jesus' sake, that the life also of Jesus might be made manifest in our mortal flesh.

"So then death worketh in us but life in you" (2 Cor. iv: 10-12).

There is yet another experimental phase of the truth of Divine Healing. Well and sound people who indeed have never been sick have dedicated their bodies to the Lord and in solemn covenant have taken Him to be their Healer. Such persons testify to a remarkable rejuvenation of constitutional vitality and reinvigoration of physical strength. Indeed, in practical experience the life of Christ imparted to our physical frames by the power of the Holy Spirit works like a tonic and is in fact a supernatural elixir for body and brain.

CHRIST OUR COMING LORD.

The crowning message of the Alliance is the crowning message of the Gospel, and that is the return to earth of the Lord Jesus Christ. The Alliance believes that Jesus is coming again, and that His coming is personal, premillennial, and imminent.

The Alliance believes, furthermore, that the return of the Lord Jesus is the supreme event in a Divine programme, which embraces the present dispensation and the coming age. This Divine programme is announced in the fifteenth chapter of Acts. In the great council at Jerusalem the president, the apostle James, stated:

"Simeon hath declared how God at the first did visit the Gentiles, to take out of them a people for His name. And to this agree the words of the prophets; as it is written,

"After this I will return, and will build again the tabernacle of David, which is fallen down; and I will build again the ruins thereof, and I will set it up:

"That the residue of men might seek after the Lord, and all the Gentiles, upon whom My name is called, saith the Lord, who doeth all these things.

"Known unto God are all His works from the beginning of the world" (vss. 14-18).

In this passage of Scripture the purpose of God for the present dispensation and the coming age is declared to be threefold, namely:

The Election of the Church
The Restoration of Israel
The Salvation of the Gentiles

First, the election of the church. "God at the first did visit the Gentiles to take out of them a people for His name."

Second, the restoration of Israel. "After this I will return, and will build again the tabernacle of David, which is fallen down; and I will build again the ruins thereof, and I will set it up."

Third, the salvation of the Gentiles. "That the residue of men might seek after the Lord, and all the Gentiles, upon whom My name is called, saith the Lord, who doeth all these things."

In this Divine programme for the present and future three facts stand out with unmistakable clearness. The first fact is the order of the events. It is the order given in the verses: there can be no change. The second fact is the part of the programme to be carried out in the present dispensation and the part to be carried out in the coming age. The election of the church is the part of the programme to be carried out in the present dispensation, while the restoration

of Israel and the salvation of the Gentiles
are the parts of the programme to be carried
out in the coming age. And the third fact
is the place in the programme when the
Lord Himself returns. This is after the
election of the church and before the restoration of Israel. "After this (the visitation of the Gentiles to take out a people for
His name) I will return" (vs. 16).

A great many of the Lord's earnest and
consecrated people believe that the world is
to be brought to Christ during the present
dispensation. Through this world-wide diffusion of the Gospel, they believe, "the earth
shall be filled with the knowledge of the
glory of the Lord, as the waters cover the
sea." This glorious consummation, it is
held, will usher in the millennial reign of
righteousness and peace, after which many,
not all, believe that Christ will return in
person and set up His earthly kingdom.

But the Alliance, taking its stand firmly
on the revealed word of God, does not hold
this view. We believe that this is an elect-
ive age, when God is visiting the Gentiles,
"to take out of them a people for His
name." This is the calling of the body of

Christ, His bride, the true church of the living God. We believe, accordingly, not that the world is to be brought to Christ during the present age, but rather that Christ is to be brought to the world. Jesus said: "And this Gospel of the kingdom shall be preached in all the world for a witness unto all nations; and then shall the end come" (Matt. xxiv: 14).

This, then, is our supreme evangelistic and missionary objective: to preach the Gospel "in all the world for a witness unto all nations; and then shall the end come." And when this shall have been done, when the church has been called out and the bride is complete, then the Lord Himself will appear, take up His part of the programme and carry it out to the glorious consummation of "the new heavens and the new earth," when God shall be all and all.

How precious and glorious to have the heavenly vision. How restful and satisfying to work in harmony with the Divine programme. The personal return of Christ is the only hope of the world and the church. Morally, the world to-day is wabbling in its orbit, madly plunging towards despair and destruction.   Religiously, the professing church is rapidly approaching a state of petrifaction and putrefaction.   Moreover, the alert believer, who knows the prophetic word and reads the signs of the times, finds no encouragement to look for improvement. For, according to the Scriptures, this dispensation will end in dissolution and destruction.   But out of the wreck and ruin "we, according to His promise, look for new heavens and a new earth, wherein dwelleth righteousness."   Our hope, therefore, is not in the fading present, but in the radiant future.   Indeed, in "that blessed hope, and the glorious appearing of the great God and our Saviour Jesus Christ," we find the greatest incentive to holiness, the strongest motive for faithfulness and the highest inspiration of service.   Upon everything and over everything in our lives let us inscribe the glowing watchword:

"Unto the coming of the Lord."

A SACRED TRUST.

The writer of the Hebrews speaks of "tasting the powers of the age to come."   In its length and breadth and its height and depth this is exactly what Christian experience is. Regeneration marks the beginning of eternal life; for eternal life is not measured by quantity but characterized by quality. It is a new kind of life, Divine life, "the life of God in the soul of man." Furthermore, sanctification is a larger instalment of eternal life, a deeper work of the Holy Ghost, bringing us more and more into conformity to the image of God's dear Son. And Divine Healing is just the first breath of the resurrection quickening our mortal frames. In the words of another:

"Have we not in the Fourfold Gospel a simple, a Scriptural and a glorious gospel, as broad in its scope as it is deep and high in our personal experience? Every segment of the great circle needs every other. Every part is strengthened by the whole. Christ our Saviour is but one chord in the heavenly music. Christ our Sanctifier makes a fuller harmony. Christ our Healer adds a still richer chord. And finally Christ our Coming Lord swells the harmony until it mingles with the everlasting chorus sung round the heavenly throne.

"The church needs this fuller Gospel

to-day as an antidote to error, a remedy for failure, an answer to the cry of every human heart and an inspiration to the loftiest faith and hope and love. Shall we not take it for ourselves and then shall we not give it as a sacred trust to all within our reach and thus prove that it is indeed the whole gospel for the whole man and the whole world?"

CHAPTER IV

WHEELS WITHIN WHEELS

𝕬 GOOD bishop of one of the evangelical denominations recently said that what his church needed was not more harness but more horse! The Christian and Missionary Alliance has always had more horse than harness—a great deal more. In other words, considering the extent and variety of the work, it has very little organization. From the beginning there have been two controlling principles: first, to wait till the expansion and character of the work emphasized the need and determined the kind of organization; and second, to keep organization in strict subordination to spirituality. As a result the administrative polity of the Alliance is marked by great simplicity.

AN UNDENOMINATIONAL MOVEMENT.

From the outset it has been made unmistakably clear that in character the Alliance movement is undenominational and unsectarian.

UNOFFICIAL EXPRESSION.

In the double number of "The Word, Work and World," for August and September, 1887, the editor thus writes:

"The Christian Alliance is designed to be a simple and fraternal union of all who hold in common the fulness of Jesus in His present grace and coming glory. It is not intended in any way to be an engine of division or antagonism in the churches, but, on the contrary, to embrace Evangelical Christians of every name who hold this common faith and life. In certain circumstances, no doubt, smaller or larger bodies of earnest Christians will be led to organize independent churches for closer fellowship or more aggressive work, but in the great majority of cases its members will be found to be the most earnest, faithful, and spiritually minded people in the various evangelical churches, and no one purposes or desires to disturb their usefulness or harmony but rather to encourage them to be known as the most valued helpers of every faithful pastor and every good work. At the same time there are special truths which, just because they are opposed by many conservative Christians, need to be doubly emphasized, and there are chords of spiritual unity more deep and dear than any denominational affinities. And these truths the Alliance is called to witness to and these ties to cherish and deepen. It was born in a most blessed atmosphere of life, truth, and love, and we believe it will prove a blessing to thousands."

OFFICIAL STATEMENT.

It is gratifying to be able to record that the Christian and Missionary Alliance, after more than a quarter-century, is still ringing true to these early words of its founder. For the official Manual of the united Society states: "It is not a sect, but a fraternal union of Christians of all evangelical denominations in cordial sympathy with all branches of the Church of Christ."

The present organization of the Alliance is a natural evolution, marked by three clearly defined stages:

THE SEPARATE SOCIETIES.

The first stage:

THE CHRISTIAN ALLIANCE.

The first organization of this society, effected in 1887, consisted of a National Association "with subordinate branches in the several states or other large sections of the country, and provision ultimately for a larger international organization so soon as it shall be deemed expedient and reasonable." The general officers, having oversight of the entire work, were a president, honorary vice-presidents, a corresponding secretary, a recording secretary, a treasurer, and an executive committee consisting of from seven to twelve members. The official business of the society was vested in the executive committee. Membership was by card issued from headquarters by the president or secretary. For ten years this simple organization was most efficient.

THE INTERNATIONAL MISSIONARY ALLIANCE.

The first organization of this society, effected also in 1887, was likewise simple and strong. The administration of its affairs was under a Board of Management, consisting of thirteen members, the general officers being a president, honorary vice-presidents, a corresponding secretary, a recording sec-

retary and a treasurer. It was provided
that:

"The Board shall appoint the missionaries employed, and exercise general su-
pervision over all the interests of the Alliance; but any local auxiliary may, with
the approval of the Board, select a special field or laborer to sustain in whole or
in part, as may be mutually arranged with
the General Board."

From time to time afterwards some modi-
fications, involving a few new features, were
made without changing the general character and extreme simplicity of the primitive organization. One important act was
the creation of an Advisory Board, consisting of fifty persons and meeting semi-
annually, for the purpose of conferring with
the General Board about all the important
interests of the Society and of offering such
suggestions and counsels respecting the
work as they may deem best. Out of this
body grew the Annual Advisory Council.

THE CONSOLIDATED SOCIETY.

The second stage:

The consolidation and incorporation of
the two separate societies into the Christian

and Missionary Alliance, consummated in 1897, called for a revised and enlarged statement of constitutional and administrative principles for the united Society. In the main this followed closely along the lines of the original organization, such new provisions being added as the expansion and development of the work demanded. Many of these remain in force. Three sections may be stated:

EVANGELISTIC AND MISSION WORK AT HOME.

"It shall be the aim of our work—steadily pursued until its full accomplishment—to see that in every center of population in the land there is a place—ever accessible and open—where Christ's hungry children can be taught, fed, and satisfied—irrespective of all sectarian distinctions, and where lost and neglected souls can find the Saviour and a hand outstretched to lead them to Him.

"As far as practicable rescue mission work among the neglected classes and in destitute regions will be carried on, and Missions established."

FOREIGN MISSIONS.

"One great object of all our work will

ever be the immediate evangelization of
Israel and the heathen world. For this
pre-eminently every Branch and Auxiliary exists; for this every soul is saved,
sanctified and healed. Those who cannot
go can help others to go, and thus be missionaries at home. Therefore this great
work shall be constantly kept before the
minds and hearts of our people. At least
once a month a missionary meeting shall
be held in every Branch. It shall be the
crowning theme of every Convention."

CONTRIBUTIONS AND FUNDS.

"The supreme reliance of this work for
the means necessary to carry it forward
shall always be in God alone. Unscrip-
tural methods of raising money will be
strictly avoided. The free-will offerings
of God's people, and especially of our
members, will be accepted and expected.
Personal solicitations for money will not
be encouraged."

NEW CONSTITUTION.

The third stage:
The new constitution adopted at the annual meeting of the Society at Boone, Iowa,
in May, 1912, represents wheels within

wheels. But as in Ezekiel's vision, in the wheels is the Living Spirit, giving to the machinery smoothness and efficiency.

THE TWO BIG WHEELS.

One big administrative wheel is the General Council. The ultimate power of the Society is vested in its entire membership. But by them it is delegated to a General Council, meeting annually and thoroughly representative of the whole constituency. The General Council is the supreme legislative body of the Alliance.

Another big administrative wheel is the Board of Managers. The General Council does not attempt executive work. For this purpose it elects a Board of Managers, which between the annual sessions of the General Council has the authoritative control and entire direction of the Alliance. The Board consists of not less than fifteen members, one third retiring at each Annual Council, but being eligible for re-election.

The officers of the Society are a President, a Vice-president, a General Secretary, a Recording Secretary, a Treasurer, and Honorary Vice-presidents.

WHEELS WITHIN WHEELS.

The work of the Board of Managers is divided into seven special departments:

Finance Department
Educational Department
Home Department
Foreign Department
Deputational Department
Publication and Literature Department
Fraternal Relations Department

Chapter V

OUR OWN BORDERS

*A*GGRESSIVE and effective missionary operations demand a strong, sustaining Home base. As the tent cords are lengthened, the stakes must be strengthened.

UNIQUE CONVENTION SYSTEM.

A good point of vantage from which to review the Home work of the CHRISTIAN AND MISSIONARY ALLIANCE for the quarter-century is our unique Convention system. It is the simple truth to say that the Alliance was born and has grown to maturity in the atmosphere of conventions. The initial impulse of the movement was imparted in the great convocation at Old Orchard in the summer of 1887. The Old Orchard Convention of 1889 witnessed the organization of the INTERNATIONAL MISSIONARY ALLIANCE and also the CHRISTIAN ALLIANCE. And at the Easter Convention in the Gospel Tabernacle, of New York, in 1897, the consolidation of the two societies was effected.

We have national conventions, and district, state, and local conventions; regular conventions and special conventions; conventions in the city and conventions in the country; conventions in the mountains and conventions by the seashore; conventions in winter and conventions in summer,—conventions, indeed, "in season and out of season." The fact is we have contracted the convention habit. For of the Alliance it may be said, "Conventions ye have always with you."

Besides the two national conventions, at Old Orchard, Maine, in August, and in New York City, in October, there is a chain of annual conventions throughout practically the entire year in many of the principal cities of our own country and also the Dominion of Canada. Moreover, the various districts, states, and even the local branches all have their annual conventions; so that it is quite safe to say that a day does not pass that an Alliance convention, and perhaps more than one, is not in session either in the Homeland or in the Foreign field.

A DAY'S PROGRAM.

The larger annual conventions are held

for a week or even for ten days. An attractive program is presented, meeting the varied needs of the people and satisfying the diversified demands of the work. The schedule of exercises for a typical day runs as follows:

A. M.

6.30	Prayer Meeting
8.00	Workers' Meeting
9.00-10.00	Quiet Hour Service
10.00-12.00	Messages on Deeper Truth and Life

P. M.

1.30	Children's Meeting
2.00	Missionary Addresses
3.00- 5.00	Preaching, or Addresses on Spiritual Themes
5.00	Inquiry Meeting
7.00	Young People's Meeting
8.00	Evangelistic Service

Besides the regular program special meetings are arranged as the need may arise. There is always an anointing service for the sick, and a baptismal service is often held.

MISSIONARY OFFERINGS.

The earlier part of a convention is de-

MISSIONARY REST HOME. NEAR DENVER. COL.

voted to the truths of Christ our Saviour and Sanctifier; while the latter part is devoted to the truths of Christ our Healer and Coming King. The crowning feature of a convention, however, is the annual missionary offering, which is raised usually on the closing day. At the larger convocations this is generally Sunday. Mr. Simpson customarily preaches the missionary sermon.

Missionary day is always a great occasion. The offering usually is taken after the sermon, often being completed however at a later service. The money is given partly in cash but mostly in pledges. These pledges are promises made in faith and dependence upon God to pay the subscription within the year. Inasmuch as no one has ever been "dunned," it is remarkable how slight has been the shrinkage of payments within the twenty-five years.

Our missionary offerings are raised without strain and usually without much effort. For the most part the local branches and individual members of the Alliance have made careful and prayerful provision in advance, so that when the day comes they are ready without hesitation to hand in their pledges. Indeed, sometimes an enthusiastic giver cannot wait until the sermon is ended, with an outburst of praise breaking in with the announcement of his subscription. Quietly assistants collect cards which have been distributed, handing them to the leader who from time to time reads the amounts without however giving the names. When the offering is in full swing a stirring scene is presented. The audience is deeply moved with spiritual fervor. The announcement of pledges ranging from a few cents to thousands of dollars calls forth expressions of devout and joyous praise. Occasionally, led by the choir or pianist, the missionary enthusiasm finds vent in outbursts of song.

Often touching and even dramatic incidents occur. Here is an offering which represents the hard earned savings of a washerwoman. Here is a small sum which a child brings, its own money gladly given for the heathen. And here a bereaved mother sends up a bank containing a few pennies, the property of her dead boy or girl. The rank and file of our Alliance people are not rich in this world's goods, but they are rich in faith and love. For the most part their missionary offerings are the result of rigid economy and the discipline of self-denial. Often indeed they are the fruit of privation and suffering. But the gifts are entirely voluntary, made in that noble spirit of sacrifice which would gladly lay down even life itself for Jesus' sake.

The high-water mark in missionary collections was reached in 1896, when at Old Orchard in August $112,000 was raised, while in New York City in October the amount rose to over $122,000. While a very high average has been steadily maintained, at no time since then at these national conventions has so large a sum been realized. It would be a mistake however to think that because of this fact less money has been given by our people for foreign missions. On the contrary the amount raised has been larger every year. The explanation of the decrease in size of the offerings at Old Orchard and New York City is simple and sufficient. In the early years the missionary collections at these great convocations drained a large part of the country, many gifts coming from as far as the Pacific slope. Within recent years, however, since the work in many states has been more fully organized, much of the money that would otherwise go to Old Orchard or New York City, is now received at Toronto, Binghamton, Rocky Springs, Beulah Park, Nyack, and many other district and local centers throughout the country. For example, one of the recent missionary offerings at Rocky Springs (representing only a part of the Eastern District), was fully $50,000, approximating in size the present offerings at Old Orchard and the October Convention in New York. Last year the money raised by our Society by collections for the home and foreign work was over $300,000. During the quarter-century the amount from all sources and for all purposes is over $4,000,000!

No feature of our work has commanded such wide attention and received such varied explanation as the offerings for foreign missions. Many news reports (and much editorial comment in particular) have been spectacular and sensational in the extreme.

The most familiar newspaper theory is that
Mr. Simpson possesses hypnotic powers,
by means of which he throws a spell over
his audiences, influencing them against
their better judgment and often without
their knowledge at the time to contribute
money to the cause of missions. Now, that
Mr. Simpson has been naturally endowed
and supernaturally endued with exceptional pulpit and platform gifts no one would
deny. Indeed those who know him best
receive him as a preacher and leader of
prophetic insight and apostolic fervor. But
the theory of hypnotic influence as an adequate explanation of the truly extraordinary missionary offerings that have marked
the history of the Alliance falls of its own
weight. Hypnotic power or even personal
magnetism might indeed sufficiently account for an occasional large missionary offering. Without interruption, however, for
twenty-five years, in the same places and
to a large extent among the same people,
the same thing has been witnessed! No;
the explanation of our extraordinary missionary offerings is found not in the human leader but in the Divine Lord. More

particularly, the explanation is fivefold:

1. The firm belief that the heathen are lost.

2. The firm belief that through the knowledge of Christ alone can the heathen be saved.

3. The conviction that we are trustees of the Gospel, responsible to give the saving knowledge of Christ to the heathen world.

4. Systematic teaching in the principles and practice of Christian giving.

5. Willingness to sacrifice for the cause of foreign missions.

EARLY BEGINNINGS.

From New York City as a radiating center the work of the Alliance has slowly but steadily reached nearly every part of our own country and large sections of Canada. From the sparsely settled districts of upper New York state to the mountain settlements of the southland our workers, both official and unofficial, are preaching the glorious truths of the Fourfold Gospel and ministering to the varied needs of diversified communities. As early as 1888 Mr. Simpson with a strong staff of helpers by invitation visited many of the larger cities of our own country and Canada. Everywhere conventions were held, often in evangelical churches, and the fourfold Gospel was proclaimed in its fulness. In many places "after services" were held, which developed into regular weekly meetings for the promotion of the distinctive truth and special testimony of the Alliance. In this way companies of believers called Branches sprang up all over the land. It was not long before the work was organized by states. Ohio was the pioneer, in 1889, closely followed however by New York, Michigan, Pennsylvania, and other states, and also by Western Ontario. Some states geographically associated were grouped into districts. Thus gradually a network of Alliance organizations, local, state and district, was spread throughout the length and breadth of the land.

LATER DEVELOPMENTS AND STATISTICAL EXHIBIT.

The story of the twenty-five years is a record of steady development and constant progress. Following is a brief statistical exhibit of the work in the Homeland:

New England District—15 branches; 10

regular meetings held without organization.

Canadian District—5 branches; 5 workers.

Eastern District—75 branches; about 70 workers; 20 regular meetings held without organization.

Central District—20 branches; 35 workers; 10 regular meetings held without organization.

Southern District—25 branches; 20 workers; 10 regular meetings held without organization.

Western District—15 branches; 10 workers; 15 regular meetings held without organization.

Pacific Coast District—20 branches; 18 workers; 12 regular meetings held without organization.

The above exhibit, however, is not complete; for, including unofficial workers and pastors of affiliated independent churches over a thousand names could be enrolled upon the Alliance roster. The entire membership of the movement has not been tabulated.

SPIRITUAL RESULTS.

But no statistical exhibit can compass the bounds of the Alliance. Figures cannot measure spiritual forces. Far beyond the limits of our organized work there is an ùnregistered constituency of whose very existence in many instances the heavenly Father alone knoweth. Moreover, the spiritual results of the past twenty-five years it would be impossible to estimate. Indeed, the number of people who have been reached and blessed by the proclamation of the Fourfold Gospel through the multiplied agencies of our Society eternity alone will reveal. The. wonderful message of Christ our Saviour has found innumerable souls darkened and burdened by sin and has brought them light and peace. The glorious message of Christ our Sanctifier has brought liberty and rest to many a bound and struggling heart. The precious message of Christ our Healer has given health to numberless sick bodies and imparted Divine vigor to countless exhausted frames. And the inspiring message of Christ our coming Lord has infused new hope and fresh strength into the heart of many a weary and discouraged worker. Nor is this all. Through the full Gospel message of the Alliance, both from the platform and in the printed page, thousands have found the Bible a new book, while hundreds of pulpits have been clothed with living power and Divine authority. The grace of God has sweetened trial, the joy of the Lord has dispelled sorrow, and the comfort of the Holy Ghost has removed the sting of bereavement.

A GRAPHIC PICTURE.

The president of the Society has drawn a graphic picture of the faithful band of home workers:

"The quiet, normal and unceasing labor of our local superintendents and evangelists in their respective fields is undoubtedly the strongest factor in all our work. The patient, self-sacrificing labor of these beloved brethren, who with inadequate support and insufficient help in their widely scattered fields, bravely toil on, often unrecognized and unpraised, constitutes the noblest sacrifice of our entire work. Often a husband and wife will be found eking out a bare living in one or two small rooms with an uncertain income, sometimes not exceeding two or three dollars a week, and counting it their greatest joy when their local convention winds up with a missionary offering of several hundred dollars and perhaps little thought of the humble workers who have sacrificed so much to bring all this about. This is the real secret of our missionary work, and the deep pathos that lies back of it should touch our hearts." And again: "Our brethren do not stand in the place of publicity or popularity. They do not minister to thronging crowds or shine in the records of the public press, but among little companies of humble followers of Christ, amid much sacrifice and self-denial, they live and labor for Christ, and, unnoticed and unpraised, gather jewels for the crowning day. We know of no work which represents so large a gathering out, not only from the world, but from the worldly church, OUT AND OUT, of so many simple-hearted, self-sacrificing and wholly consecrated followers of the meek and lowly Jesus. We thank God for the beautiful Christian lives that God has given us in the fellowship of the Alliance."

INDEPENDENT CHURCHES.

About a dozen years ago the unfounded charge was frequently made that the Alliance was a proselyting agency. In consequence, a mighty cry went up to heaven from our people for souls and for soul-winners. . The Lord answered this cry. Our workers were clothed afresh with an evangelistic spirit, and the branches began to pray and labor anew for the salvation of the lost. More than before regular Alliance meetings closed with altar services, and many souls were saved. Conversions became a marked feature of the conventions. Homes were opened for meetings in the outskirts of cities and villages, and evangelistic services were held in sparsely settled country districts.

Thus a new situation was created, out of which developed a difficult and delicate problem. This problem was in part rural and in part urban.

In cities and villages in many instances it was found not to be a happy arrangement to send our converts to the churches for baptism. Indeed, our people were often made to feel that not only for the ordinance of baptism but also for the observance of the Lord's Supper they were not welcome in the churches. In these circumstances the Board considered it wise, where the conditions were ripe and the need was urgent, to encourage the branches to effect a simple New Testament church organization. In a number of places this was done.

In the country the situation was somewhat different. In many sparsely settled districts Christians were found without church homes and children without Sunday School privileges. In such places Sunday Schools were organized, and regular Sunday services established. Out of these conditions in some instances churches grew up. They became, in fact, a necessity; for the field was unoccupied, none of the Evangelical denominations ministering to the spiritual destitution of the people.

There are to-day throughout the entire country about fifty independent Full Gospel churches in association with the Alliances. These churches, it must be clearly understood, are not Alliance churches. There is, in fact, no such thing as an Alliance church. Nor indeed can there be, for

the CHRISTIAN AND MISSIONARY ALLIANCE
is not a denominational body nor in any
wise a sectarian movement. How these independent churches are affiliated with our
organization has been explained in an earlier chapter.

PUBLICATION INTERESTS.

The publication interests have always
been, so to speak, the strong right arm of
the work. From the very beginning indeed
the preached word and the printed page
have gone hand in hand together. The
successor of "Word, Work and World" was
the "Christian and Missionary Alliance," a
weekly paper which made its first appearance in January, 1888. It has been issued
continuously since that time, its name now
being "The Alliance Weekly, a Journal of
Christian Life and Missions." Mr. Simpson is editor, assisted by an able corps of
associate editors and an efficient staff of
special contributors. It is impossible to
estimate the literally world-wide influence
of this deeply spiritual paper, which is now
read regularly by over fifty thousand people. It is daily food to multitudes of hungry hearts. Its pages have been "leaves of

healing" to innumerable sick bodies and exhausted frames. It has brought inspiration to countless discouraged workers. Through its influence ministers all over the country, and indeed throughout the world, have been clothed with a new Divine authority, their messages being freighted with freshness, fragrance and fruitfulness.

Besides issuing the weekly paper the Alliance has published a large number of books and tracts. A few years ago a Colportage Library of about thirty volumes had a wide circulation. Mr. Simpson himself has written more than fifty books, besides many tracts, in which are unfolded the doctrinal teaching and special testimony of the Alliance. Both by the paper and through his books, as well as in the pulpit and on the platform, Mr. Simpson ministers to a world-wide constituency. Indeed, as a spiritual expounder of the Gospel of the Fulness of Jesus he has probably no superior living. Many of his books have passed through several editions, and have been of unspeakable blessing to countless hungry hearts. A song book, "Hymns of the Christian Life," made its appearance a number of years ago, and is used in all our conventions, most of the branches, and in many churches. A goodly proportion of the hymns, both words and tunes, were composed by Mr. Simpson.

INSTITUTIONAL WORK.

While the Alliance is primarily and essentially a spiritual movement, yet of necessity its activities, in the homeland as well as on the foreign field, have in many instances taken institutional form. Some of the early institutions have passed away with the immediate and pressing emergency that gave them birth, while others have grown larger and stronger with the expansion and consolidation of the movement.

Of the former class of institutions two merit historic mention: Berachah Orphanage and the Home School.

BERACHAH ORPHANAGE.

For a number of years this work was carried on at College Point, Long Island, where a little monthly paper, "Echoes from the Valley of Berachah," was issued. Later the institution was removed to Nyack. The orphanage was finally closed because the boys found self-supporting positions, while the girls entered Christian homes. The early years of this work tell a story of faith, love, and sacrifice.

HOME SCHOOL.

After the Missionary Institute was removed to Nyack, there was carried on at headquarters, 690 Eighth Avenue, New York City, a Training School for Home Workers. Through the fall, winter, and spring months it offered several "Six Weeks' Courses in Essentials." The teaching staff was strong and spiritual, while the instruction and training were varied and practical. Only recently and largely for financial reasons was the Home School closed and its work merged into the Nyack educational system. Some of the best home workers were trained in this institution.

EDUCATIONAL SYSTEM.

Of the present institutional work of the Alliance in the country by far the largest and most important is our educational system. By the providence of God the Alliance has undertaken the secondary and in part collegiate education of its youth and the training of young men and young wom-

en for the home work and the mission field.
At Ayr, North Carolina, and at Boydton,
Virginia, successful schools, in part secondary and in part Biblical, are carried on for
colored young people. At Toccoa, Geor-
gia, and at Boone, Iowa, are growing institutions of great promise, which offer
courses in both secondary education and
Biblical training.

But the crown of our educational system
is at Nyack, New York, whose two coedu-
cational schools, the Wilson Memorial
Academy and the Missionary Training Institute, have been officially recognized by
the Annual Council as the central and national institutions of the Alliance. The
work is carried on in two divisions: Academic and Biblical, the entire system being
under the administration of a Board of
Trustees.

The younger of the schools, the Wilson
Memorial Academy, was founded in 1906,
being originally called the "Nyack Seminary," but later taking the name of its first
President, the late Doctor Henry Wilson.
It maintains Grammar work of the seventh
and eighth grades, regular four years' High

School work with classical, scientific and commercial courses, and a full freshman year of college work. In every subject in both Academic and Collegiate departments the work is held carefully to the recognized standards of scholarship. The requirements of the New York State Board of Regents are met in every course. "It is recognized that the Grammar and High Schools of our land are without spiritual safeguards and are rapidly becoming such as to undermine the faith and even endanger, through their indiscriminate student life, the morals of our boys and girls. The Academy has arisen in answer to the prayers of thousands of parents and the call of a host of earnest Christian young people. It stands as a protest against the unbelieving, unspiritual educational systems of our day. It is indeed called to show how it is possible to combine thorough instruction and high scholarship with simple faith and consecrated living."

The older of the Nyack Schools, the Missionary Training Institute, is now in its thirty-first year. Thus it antedates by several years the organization of the CHRIS-

TIAN AND MISSIONARY ALLIANCE. Its first class was graduated in 1884. At present the Institute offers three courses, namely: a one year Christian Workers' Course, a full two year Biblical and missionary course, and a one year Post-Graduate course with subjects largely of a theological character. "From the beginning the Institute has been one of the foundations of the work. It has always stood for loyalty to the Word of God, spiritual fervor, and intelligent missionary zeal. From the strong and wholesome atmosphere of the Institute its students have gone forth to man nearly every post in our home and foreign work, and to respond to many a Divine call outside our ranks, carrying with them the full Gospel by lives unreservedly devoted to God."

Chapter VI

THE ENDS OF THE EARTH

A S is expressed by the name of the movement, THE CHRISTIAN AND MISSIONARY ALLIANCE has two great objects, namely: the experience of the fulness of Jesus for spirit, soul and body and the immediate evangelization of the heathen world.

THE SUPREME OBJECTIVE

Three striking facts connected with the beginning of the ALLIANCE show that its supreme objective is foreign missions. The controlling purpose and dominant note of the first Old Orchard Convention in 1887 was the speedy proclamation of the Gospel to the ends of the earth. Again, the INTERNATIONAL MISSIONARY ALLIANCE was incorporated a year earlier than the CHRISTIAN ALLIANCE. Finally, the INTERNATIONAL MISSIONARY ALLIANCE was organized for the specific purpose of carrying the Gospel to Tibet, then an unopened and inaccessible country. This indeed has been from the beginning the in-

spiring and moulding purpose of the Society
—to plant the banner of the cross in unoccupied and neglected mission lands. This was
Paul's supreme missionary objective (Romans 15, 20).

MISSIONARY OBLIGATION

The supreme missionary objective of the
ALLIANCE rests upon the solid Scriptural
foundation of missionary obligation. This is
fourfold:

First.—We believe that the heathen are sit-
ting in darkness and in the region and shadow
of death. Moreover, we believe that the
heathen world is lost. This is an awful belief,
it is true; but the ALLIANCE holds it because
it is clearly and unmistakably taught in the
Word of God (Luke 19:10; Romans 3:
10-26).

Second.—We believe that the heathen who
are lost, having no hope and without God in
the world, can be saved only through faith
in the Lord Jesus Christ (Acts 4, 12; 16, 31;
Romans 10:9, 10).

Third.—We believe that the Lord's people
are under the most solemn obligation, as a
simple matter of duty, to give the knowledge
of Christ and His fulness to the heathen. We

are, we hold, trustees of the Gospel. Indeed, with Paul the ALLIANCE can say:

"I am debtor both to the Greeks and to the barbarians; both to the wise and the unwise. So, as much as in me is I am ready to preach the Gospel" (Romans 1:14, 15).

Fourth.—We believe that the speedy evangelization of the world will bring the glad day of Christ's return. For this we labor and pray and wait (Matthew 24:14; 1 Thessalonians 1:9, 10).

DISTINCTIVE MISSIONARY PRINCIPLES

A few years ago the President of the ALLIANCE gave the following expression to its distinctive missionary principles:

"1. The work is projected from the premillennial standpoint. We believe in the personal return of the Lord Jesus Christ and that the evangelization of the world is the best way to hasten His coming. According to the programme so clearly marked out in the fifteenth chapter of the Acts of the Apostles, the Lord is visiting the Gentiles in this dispensation to take out of them a people for His name and when this shall have been accomplished, we may expect the Lord's immediate return, the restoration of Israel and the

opening of the millennial age.   We believe
that the Gospel is to be preached 'in all the
world as a witness unto all nations and then
shall the end come.'   So far from paralyzing
missionary effort this blessed hope has been
found to be a most powerful and practical
incentive to it.

"2. The ALLIANCE emphasizes the special
agency and superintendency of the Holy
Ghost in the work of missions, seeking only
for wholly consecrated missionaries and holding the work under the constant direction of
the Spirit of God.   It goes without saying
that the testimony of the ALLIANCE is a full
Gospel and the converts of our missions are
led to know the Lord Jesus in His fulness
and expect the baptism of the Holy Spirit.

"3. Along with this it naturally follows that
the work should be a work of faith and that
it should be maintained by a spirit of prayer
and continual dependence upon God.   Having
no ecclesiastical constituency the workers on
the field and the executive officers at home
are led to look more directly to God for all
their resources and supplies.

"4. The ALLIANCE missionary work is
evangelistic and aggressive rather than edu-

cational and institutional. We do not attempt to establish educational institutions, and transplant our denominational organizations to heathen soil, but to give the Gospel as rapidly as possible to all races and tongues. [In principle this continues to be the settled policy of the Society. However, in some countries, as Palestine and India, orphanages have been established, while on a growing number of fields training schools for native workers are carried on.]

"5. Our chosen fields are the 'regions beyond,' the unoccupied portions of the heathen world, and so our missionaries have been led into the most difficult and remote regions, and enabled to introduce the Gospel to many sections where Christ had not been named, such as Kwang-Si in South China, the province of Hunan in Central China, the borders of Tibet [and recently the country of Annam], the tribes of Mongolia, the unoccupied region of the Congo and the Niger in Africa and some of the neglected republics of South America.

"6. The principle of economy is rigidly aimed at. The expenses of home administration are reduced to the lowest possible figure. Missionaries on the field are not promised regular salaries, but simply their expenses, and all the workers unite to make the means at our disposal accomplish the largest possible results without really sacrificing or crippling the work. [Monthly allowances sufficient to meet actual needs are granted the missionaries. From time to time these allowances are increased as the cost of living in different countries is raised.]

"7 The principle of sacrifice is the deepest element in our work. Again and again it has been displayed upon the field by the missionaries themselves, and not less by the self-sacrificing gifts of those who sustain them at home."

MISSIONARY STATISTICS

The following are the latest available missionary statistics of the ALLIANCE:

Fields   17
Stations   101
Outstations   187
Missionaries   263
Native workers   386
Organized churches..................   77
Communicants 5,217
Baptized (1912)....................   600
Enrolled inquirers 1,360

Sunday schools 107
Scholars in Sunday schools............6,900
Primary day schools.................. 127
Middle boarding schools............. 9
Scholars in boarding schools.......... 237
Bible training schools................ 10
Students in training schools.......... 105
Native offerings (1912).........$ 10,589.11
School fees collected (1912)..... 2,560.25
Value of mission property....... 275,000.00

WORK IN MISSION LANDS

Within the compass of a single chapter it
is impossible to attempt to give anything like
a complete account of the foreign missionary
work of the ALLIANCE during the quarter century. At most only an outline sketch of each
field can be presented.

In 1893 Mr. Simpson made a tour of visitation of our mission fields, with the exception
of Africa and South America. His journeys
through the Orient marked an epoch in our
missionary history, the presence and counsel
of the president of the Society bringing inspiration and helpfulness to all our own missionaries as well as to many missionaries of
other Boards. Out of Mr. Simpson's letters
to the ALLIANCE grew "Larger Outlooks on

Missionary Lands," an illustrated volume full of information and inspiration. From time to time the Board of Managers has sent several of its officers on deputational visits to foreign lands. Recently Mr. Simpson made a tour of visitation of the West Indies and several of our mission fields in South America.

In the record of our Missionary history mention must be made of Mrs. A. B. Simpson. For years, besides being a member of the Board of Managers, she was Financial Secretary and also Secretary of Missionary Appointment and Equipment. Mrs. Simpson is indeed the mother of the ALLIANCE. To her faith and love, her self-sacrifice and prayer the progress and efficiency of the entire movement have been in goodly measure due.

A bird's-eye view of our various mission fields will now be attempted.

PALESTINE

"Beginning at Jerusalem" is the Divine order.

At present there are three stations: Jerusalem, Hebron and Beersheba. The staff consists of fourteen missionaries and fourteen native workers.

The ALLIANCE Mission in Palestine was

opened in 1890. The pioneer missionaries were Miss Lucy Dunn, of Pittsburgh, and Miss Eliza Robinson, of the Gospel Tabernacle, New York. Their home in Hebron soon became the center of such deep and widespread spiritual influences that they became known as "the women who live next door to God." A little later came the Cruikshanks and the Murrays, who helped to lay the foundations of solid missionary work. In 1899 Mr. and Mrs. Senft visited our Palestine mission and were instrumental in the erection of an Iron Gospel Tabernacle in Jerusalem. This was dedicated Easter, 1904, and here General William Booth, of the Salvation Army, held a series of evangelistic services, during which sixty were converted. In 1906 the American Free Church was organized, and Easter of the present year a beautiful stone church was dedicated, the value of the property being $25,-000. The ALLIANCE has the only American mission in Jerusalem, and already our new church has become the center alike of English speaking worshipers and of aggressive evangelistic work. The church supports an evangelist in China, and the Sunday school a teacher in the Congo mission.

The appointment of the Rev. A. E. Thompson as Superintendent, in 1903, marked a new epoch in our Palestine mission. The work being accomplished is evangelistic and educational. By itinerating tours the Gospel is carried to widely distant parts of the country. The people reached are mostly Jews and Moslems, including Syrians, Arabs and Armenians, including some Roman Catholics. Work among the Jews is hindered from the fact that new converts to Christianity lose caste among their people. Bibles and tracts, in thirteen different languages and dialects, are distributed.

In 1897 a training school for girls was opened in Jaffa. This has recently been removed to Jerusalem. At present forty girls are in attendance, one-fourth Jewesses and the rest Moslems, Catholics and a few Protestants. A training school for boys in Jerusalem has graduated two classes. A new theological school for native evangelists, ministers and missionaries has recently been opened in Jerusalem.

In prophecy and history the Holy Land has always been the pivotal country. "Palestine is in transition, customs, ideals, aspirations are

changing. Intolerance and exclusiveness are
no longer universal. The right of individual
liberty of conscience is recognized by some.
The desire for Western culture and prosperity
is causing many to risk religious contamina-
tion. Men have not yet become irreligious, as
they have in Japan. Christian meetings are
now openly attended by Jews and Moslems.
Every mission school is overflowing. Missionaries are received, if not welcomed, when
they visit Moslem villages. Everywhere doors
are opening. In the occupied centers there is
increased freedom for aggressive work. There
are still neglected districts on this side of
Jordan, and but two small mission stations in
the trans-Jordanic country. Beyond lies Arabia, still untouched, already pierced by the
Mecca Railway, now open from Damascus to
Mecca. The opportunity long waited for has
come."

<h3 style="text-align:center">INDIA</h3>

The ALLIANCE missions are in the Western
part, in the provinces of Berar, Khandesh and
Gujerat. There are twenty-two stations,
seventeen outstations, seventy-seven missionaries and ninety-five native workers.

In 1888 Miss Helen Dawlly, and a little

later Miss Carrie B. Bates, with two other young ladies, went to India and labored in connection with an independent work of the Rev. M. B. and Mrs. Fuller, at Akola, Berar. In 1892 the ALLIANCE took over the North Berar Mission, and the same year a party of sixteen missionaries went out with the Fullers to the new field. The following year there were forty-seven missionaries in India. In 1894 a number of stations were opened in Khandesh and Gujerat.

Until recently an English work was carried on in the city of Bombay, where Berachah Home, a receiving sttaion for new missionaries and an institution for rest and healing, was for many years located.

Extending from 200 to 450 miles east of Bombay is the Marathi field, divided into the two districts of Khandesh and Berar. The people are mostly farmers, proud and exclusive, and it is their boast that they have never yielded to foreign influence. To the north of Bombay 280 miles is the Gujerati field. It is a pastoral district, and the people are simple and more open to the Gospel than the Marathi.

Because of the frequent and terrible ravages of famine in India a prominent place in missionary effort must be given to orphanage work. At Kaira and Khamgaon the ALLI-ANCE has orphanages for girls, and at Dholka and Akola, in connection with flourishing industrial work, orphanages for boys, 300 children being in the four institutions. Some years ago during a severe famine *The Christian Herald,* of New York, supported 250 children in our orphanages. The membership of our native churches has largely been recruited from the orphanages. Difficult in all mission fields, missionary statistics are particularly difficult in India. After fifteen years of ALLIANCE work there was a native church membership of fifteen hundred. In 1907 our Indian mission (and in particular the orphanages) was visited by the wonderful revival which, beginning in Wales and England, swept over many countries and touched our own shores. The fruit of this remarkable work of grace is still being gathered. In fact, India is to-day more open to the Gospel than ever before. The native church has been spiritually quickened, especially among the higher classes, heathen hearts have been Divinely softened, and on every hand the missionaries are meeting a more friendly spirit and finding more open doors than, without increased and immediate reinforcements, they can enter.

A few years ago our Indian mission decided to emphasize the importance of station and itinerating *evangelism* as the foundation of permanent missionary work. To this end the training of native workers was found to be essential. Accordingly, two important Biblical and Theological Schools for this purpose have already been established, chiefly through the generous gift of Mr. D. B. Strouse of Salem, Va.

The India Alliance, a monthly paper, has for years been an invaluable agency in all our varied missionary work. Of our earlier missionaries one name stands out above all others. It is not too much to say that the life and labors of Mrs. Jennie Fuller have left a lasting impress on India. Her "Wrongs of Indian Womanhood," a missionary classic, has done much toward ameliorating the condition of native women.

CHINA

In the empire, now the republic, of China the ALLIANCE has mission stations in the provinces of Kwang-si, Anhuei, Hunan, Hupeh, Kansu, and adjacent borders of Tibet and the city of Shanghai. In all there are twenty-six stations, thirty-five outstations, ninety-two missionaries, and 143 native workers. This varied exhibit represents the work of four different missions, namely: South China, West China and Tibet, Central China and the city of Shanghai.

CENTRAL CHINA

This mission occupies the three inland provinces of Anhuei, Hunan and Hupeh. There are eight stations, thirteen outstations, forty-one missionaries, and fifty-two native workers.

This field is somewhat unwieldy for the most effective missionary work, spreading out in several wings from the city of Wuhu in Anhuei and the cities of Hankow and Wu Chang in Hupeh. The station nearest to the sea coast and the station farthest from the sea coast are as wide apart as New York and St. Louis. In general the territory follows the course of the Yang-Tse River, and the constituency which the Mission seeks to reach with the Gospel numbers about 7,000,000 people.

Central China is our oldest Mission in China. It was opened in 1890. The first appointed missionary was the Rev. William Cassidy, who died from smallpox while *en route* to his post. In 1894 a commodious Receiving Home for new missionaries while engaged in language study and for annual conferences was built in Wuhu, the headquarters. Hunan, the most anti-foreign of China's eighteen provinces, was the last to permit the missionary—the hated "foreign devil"—to enter and remain. But in 1896 "three of our missionaries—Brown, Alexander and Chapin—were honored of God to be among the pioneers of Hunan and to endure no little rough treatment and danger for Christ's sake." In Chang-teh in November, 1897, these brethren opened the *first Protestant Mission Station* in Hunan. Now the ALLIANCE has three stations in three of the largest cities of Hunan. In Chang-teh a Boys' School has recently been started. In 1908 a training school for native workers was opened in Wuchang, the new headquarters. In 1909 a gracious revival visited several of our mission stations.*

According to the latest statistics, in our Central China Mission there are over four

---

*From the mission comes a ringing Macedonian cry for help.

hundred communicants. Eight Sunday schools have an attendance of 579 children. Eleven primary schools teach 249 scholars. Two middle schools had sixty students, until closed by the recent revolution.

SOUTH CHINA

This mission occupies the southern province of Kwang-si. There are ten stations, fifteen outstations, thirty-six missionaries, and fifty-five native workers.

Kwang-si is a compact, mountainous and hostile province, somewhat larger than the New England States, and with a population of 6,000,000, or about equal to that of the Dominion of Canada.

The ALLIANCE secured a foothold in South China or the Portuguese island of Macao in 1893. Two years later, in 1895, the province of Kwang-si was entered. "Upon the CHRISTIAN AND MISSIONARY ALLIANCE the Lord conferred the honor and privilege of having the first permanent resident missionaries within Kwang-si's hostile borders, and to our missionaries even yet has been left the great bulk of the work of evangelizing this whole province. Our workers have braved the hardships of pioneer work and primitive modes of travel and life, have endured insult and ill-treatment on their lonely inland stations, and have stood firm at their posts of danger when infuriated mobs have gathered at the chapel doors and attempted to tear down the premises." Continuing the story Mr. Oldfield says: "During the seventeen or eighteen years that have followed our earliest occupation, many itinerating trips have been made through the various portions of the province, Gospels and tracts have been scattered and much preparatory work done.   In spite of hardships and trials incident to pioneer missionary work, the Lord has blessed our mission abundantly and set His seal upon its labors."

Wuchow, the headquarters of our mission, was opened in 1907.   Here in 1909 an attractive chapel was built.   The native church is entirely self-supporting, having a strong staff of local workers.   More recently two Bible training schools for native workers have been opened and have already sent out many consecrated men and women.   A girls' school has also been erected.   An excellent printing plant, which puts out a Full-Gospel magazine in Chinese, also issues the SOUTH

CHINA ALLIANCE TIDINGS, a monthly paper of great value in carrying on our missionary work. In 1908 the great revival wave visited many of the stations.

According to the latest available statistics in the South China field "there are eleven native churches with a membership of 701. Besides the 153 baptisms reported there are 182 inquirers, 390 in Sunday schools, 297 in primary schools, 58 in higher schools and 26 under special training for missionary work." Tidings come that unless Kwang-Si is fully occupied at once part of the territory will be lost to another society.

WEST CHINA AND TIBET

This mission occupies the far northwestern province of Kansu and Amdo, the north-eastern province of Tibet. There are seven stations, nine outstations, fourteen missionaries and nineteen native workers.

The province of Kansu has a high elevation and is difficult of access. "It is reached by a hard, tedious journey, partly by river and partly overland, and consuming three months from Hankow." All our Mission Stations along the China-Tibetan border are located in the valley of the Tao River, which empties into the Yellow River thirty-five miles west of Lanchow, the capital of Kansu.

The ALLIANCE entered Kansu in 1904. In that year *Chone* was opened, and now has a small church and a girls' day school. In 1905 *Tihtao* was opened. Here our Mission owns a fine property, comprising a church of sixty members and a promising Bible Training School, started in 1908, by the late Rev. David P. Ekvall. *Minchow* was opened in 1906, and has a native church of sixty members, fifteen of whom are women. And the same year *Taochow* (new city) was permanently opened by the late Miss Effie Gregg. Here a church building has been erected to her memory and also to the memory of Mrs. Frank Baer (neé Ruth Lindberg) who, after nursing Miss Gregg through her fatal illness of smallpox, contracted the dread disease and died.

About twenty years ago the late Rev. David W. Lelacheur was appointed Superintendent of our missions in China. On an extraordinary pioneer tour attended by great danger and extreme hardship he penetrated to *Chone*, across the borders of hostile Tibet. He visited the Lamasery of Darge and prayed that God would give the ALLIANCE this heathen temple for the preaching of the Gospel. At the time it seemed that such a prayer could not be answered in our lifetime, but "with God all things are possible" and "all things are possible to him that believeth." However, the property is now possessed by our Mission, along with thirty acres of land attached, and has appropriately been called the *"Lelacheur Memorial."* The headquarters of our Tibetan work is at Taochow (old city), an important commercial border town, where we have a promising church and a girls' boarding-school.

Our Tibetan work, begun in 1905, is largely among Mohammedans. Recently the Mission was visited by a most gracious revival, which resulted in the conversion of many sinners and spiritual quickening and strengthening of the native churches.

"Formerly we had considerable work in northern Shansi, carried on by our Swedish brethren; and a women's work at Pekin, under the leadership of Miss Duow. During the Boxer uprising of 1900 these Swedish Missions were broken up, and more than thirty of our precious workers and their little ones died the death of martyrs. As yet

the Board has not seen its way clear to re-
open the work in these parts."

SHANGHAI

In the city of Shanghai, the important
central port of China, there is an aggressive
work being carried on among English-speak-
ing Chinese and also the sailors of American
and European men-of-war, always in port.
The work is in charge of Mr. and Mrs.
Woodberry with four missionaries and seventeen native helpers. Besides Beulah Home,
there is a church of sixty members, a Sunday
school of 120 and day schools numbering
about 140 scholars. Our Shanghai Mission
owns a valuable property consisting of two
fine houses erected in 1909 at a cost of about
$20,000.

In 1902 Mr. and Mrs. Woodberry made a
long and difficult journey through Shensi to
settle the Society's claim for indemnity in
connection with the lives and losses sustained
by our Swedish Mission.

ANNAM

This is our youngest mission field. The
great kingdom of Annam was only recently
opened by some of our South China workers.
The city of Touraine has been occupied and

the adjacent district is being evangelized.
Our ALLIANCE work is the only Protestant
Mission among 20,000,000 heathen. Already
many are interested in the Gospel, and one
has been baptized. Four or five cities are
ready to receive missionaries. Money is coming in for Annam and reinforcements are being sent.

JAPAN

The ALLIANCE Mission in Japan comprises
one station, three outstations, nine missionaries and nine native workers. Our work is
located in the city and province of Hiroshima,
about twelve hours' ride from Kobe.

In 1891 Miss Helen Kinney opened an
orphanage in Japan. Another pioneer missionary was Miss Emma Barns. Dr. Gulick was
appointed Superintendent in 1893. During
these two decades our mission work has
passed through many vicissitudes. Some stations, once occupied, have been abandoned.
A new and commodious chapel is about
to be erected in Hiroshima. In the city
of Hiroshima we have a most encouraging work. Mr. Lindstrom says: "God has
again opened the door for Bible classes among

students in Hiroshima, and several of these young men have already decided for Christ. Our Gospel meetings in the halls of Hiroshima are well attended, and the people are ready to listen. Our Sunday morning services are largely attended and deeply spiritual. The Sunday evening Gospel meetings are well advertised by a band of enthusiastic young believers walking through the streets behind a big drum, and carrying lanterns and banners to lead the way to the Mission. A great number of children attend Sunday school, and are the real hope of the future church. Seven young men attend our training class for native workers. Cheering tidings have come to us from Shobara, one of our outstations, of revived interest there. Finally, when our new chapel shall be opened during this year, we expect the people of Hiroshima to take a much greater interest in the work and that many souls shall be saved." In 1906 a revival swept over Japan, quickening and strengthening our Mission.

The present statistics show a native church membership of 179, Sunday school scholars numbering 400, a day school with forty-five in attendance, besides seven in the training school for native workers.

PHILIPPINE ISLANDS

The ALLIANCE Mission in the Philippine Islands comprises one station, twelve outstations, six missionaries and four native workers.

Our work is on the island of Mindanao, the second largest island in the Archipelago. The pioneer missionary was David McKee, who had been a soldier in the Philippines, and who began evangelistic work in 1902. His ministry was cut short by death from cholera, contracted while nursing the sick. After a break of two years Mr. and Mrs. D. O. Lund, who had been laboring among seamen, took up the work. The staff has since been increased to six.

Missionary work is carried on among the pagan aborigines, Japanese, Chinese, Mohammedans and, to a very large extent, Romanists. The work among the Romanists has encountered bitter and violent opposition, but is making steady headway.

"From Zamboanga, the headquarters, constant itinerancies are made, open air meetings held, and great quantities of Scripture por-

tions and tracts distributed from house to
house in that district and on another island
called Basilan." An automobile reaches many
interior towns; while along the coastline of
Zamboanga, 700 miles in extent and dotted
with villages containing 100,000 people, a
motorboat plies. "The people come out in
crowds to hear the 'sweet story of old.' The
interest is most encouraging, and in the different towns little groups are taking their stand
for the Lord and the Bible." A translation
of the Bible in the Moro language is nearing
completion.

The statistics of our Mission show a native
church of ninety-seven, with forty recent baptisms, a Sunday school of 150, a girls' school
numbering 100, with fourteen persons in the
training school for native workers.

AFRICA—THE SOUDAN.

The Soudan Mission comprises five stations,
three outstations, sixteen missionaries and
two native workers.

The ALLIANCE took over the "Soudan
Mission" in 1892. The name *Soudan,* however, is a misnomer, as all our work is in
the British maritime colony of *Sierre Leone.*
Freetown was for a time occupied as our

Mission headquarters. Here in the little English cemetery is buried the Rev. D. W. Lelacheur, Field Superintendent of the ALLIANCE, who died in 1901 while on a deputational visit to the Soudan.

Our present stations follow generally the course of the Rokel River, and are located in the *Timne* and *Kuranko* countries. One hundred and twenty miles inland is Makomp, the present terminus of a new railway, which makes this station the convenient headquarters of our Mission. Ten miles south of Makomp is Mayose, 140 miles inland is Masumberi. Farandugo is 200 miles inland. And Tibabadugo, the farthest inland station, is 220 miles from the coast.

The Soudan Mission is our hardest field. Indeed, along with manifest tokens of the Divine presence and gracious seasons of prosperity, it has always had a struggle for existence. The climate is most dangerous. In proportion to its size and the number of foreign workers there have been more missionary deaths than on any other field. The Soudan has indeed been called "the white man's grave." Climatic difficulties, however, are being overcome, and in recent years there have been fewer deaths among our workers. Once flourishing stations, such as Magbelle, Bethel and Benduga have been closed for lack of missionaries to man them. Language difficulties are not formidable, nor are the natives hostile. Mohammedan opposition, however, is bitter and treacherous. The problem of the Soudan is twofold: perilous climate and dearth of missionaries and trained native workers, especially men. But the problem, while perplexing, is not insoluble.

There must be a forward movement in the Soudan. The thirty lonely missionary graves emphasize the demand. Ten men and ten thousand dollars, accompanied with much prayer and mighty faith, would go far to solve the Soudan problem. Here is a challenge! Who will meet it?

Already indeed a brighter day is dawning upon the Soudan. The little band of intrepid workers has been reinforced. Fresh interest is manifested. Some stations in the Kuranko country have been reopened. A number of baptisms have occurred. One hundred and ninety attend four Sunday schools, and nineteen attend four primary schools. A little printing press has been installed, and a primer has been printed and circulated in the Timne language. On all sides the prospects are bright and encouraging.

AFRICA—THE CONGO

The Congo Mission comprises seven stations, sixty-eight outstations, twenty-five missionaries and sixty-nine native workers.

The Congo has the signal distinction of being the first field to which a band of missionaries was sent. In the fall of 1884, several years before the ALLIANCE was organized, eight young men sailed for the Congo, the fruit of the first class of the New York Missionary Training Institute. In the early years of the ALLIANCE movement several quite large parties opened up and developed the Congo field. Among the pioneer missionaries were John Condit, John and Peter Scott and William Macomber, the sainted Gospel hymn writer.

Of the seven stations in operation at present Boma, at the mouth of the Congo River, is the receiving station and headquarters of the mission. This sea coast town is a growing commercial center. Then in their order up country from Boma are the five stations of Vungu, Lolo, Kinkonzi, Maduda, and Yema.* These are all located in the lower Belgian Congo, in what is called the "Mayombe" district. The seventh station is Mboka, which is located in Portuguese territory, north of the "Mayombe" district.

The Congo is one of our best mission fields, and this in the face of a dangerous tropical climate and other perils and trying conditions paralleled only in the Soudan. Indeed, in every respect this is a singularly efficient Mission. For the first time in years one of our missionaries recently laid down his life. In fact, for a period of seven years the ranks of foreign workers was unbroken by death. This is a truly wonderful record of Divine preservation and providence and is cause for thanksgiving and praise to God.

Native living conditions in Congoland have been a reproach and disgrace to so-called Christian civilization. The white man has here made the abode of his black brother a veritable "habitation of cruelty." For the wretched people are not only the victims by natural inheritance and environment of superstition, witchcraft and idolatry, but they have

*Recently Yema and Maduda have been consolidated with Kinkonzi in a strong forward movement.

A BAPTISMAL SERVICE IN CONGO.

been made victims by European commerce and
politics of the unspeakable rubber atrocities.
However, "political conditions have improved,
and the horrors formerly reported through the
excesses of the traders and officials have
ceased for the time. But the Roman Catholics
are openly hostile, and there have been several
cases of violent assaults upon the missionaries
and native Christians by their people."

On the other hand, the Mission reports a
splendid work being carried on in the many
outstations by the seventy trained native
evangelists. There is a native church of
nearly 800 members, with not quite 100 baptisms reported for the past year. The Sunday schools are attended by 700, and about
1,400 are enrolled in the primary schools.
Last year "the contributions of our native
Christians amounted to $650, an average of
almost one dollar per member, putting to
shame the average gifts of the majority of
American Christians for Missions." Recently a gracious outpouring of the Holy
Spirit visited this field, quickening both the
missionary staff and the native church. A
number of remarkable cases of Divine Heal-

ing have occurred.   There is an imperative
need for a training school for native evangelists.

THE WEST INDIES—JAMAICA

The ALLIANCE Mission in the British colony
of Jamaica comprises two stations, three outstations, three missionaries, and two native
workers.

More than fifteen years ago Mission work
was begun on this beautiful island by Mr.
and Mrs. D. A. McKillop, and is now being
carried on by Mr. and Mrs. George H. Mc-
Clare.   The Mission has had its lights and
shadows, but is now in a prosperous condition.   There is a native church membership
of 237 in two separate congregations, and
three enrolled Sunday schools with 396 in
attendance; 100 recent converts are soon to
be baptized.

THE WEST INDIES—PORTO RICO

The ALLIANCE Mission in Porto Rico comprises ten stations, eleven outstations, three
missionaries and twenty-one native workers.

Since the Spanish-American war Porto
Rico, like the distant Philippines, is really
Home missionary territory.   "Our work on
this island is unique in this respect, that it

has from the beginning been chiefly conducted by workers who are themselves converts from the Roman church and Latin America. It is a fine example of the value and efficiency of such work." According to the statistics there is a total membership (in ten organized churches) of 341, not including twenty-one baptisms, and 129 recent converts. There is a total Sunday school enrollment of 623. Last year the offering of the native Christians was $1,108, or an average of about $3.25 per head! Four students are preparing for future service in the Mission at the Bible School in Venezuela.

THE WEST INDIES—SANTO DOMINGO

The ALLIANCE Mission in Santo Domingo comprises but one station, three outstations, one missionary and one native worker.

Although the population of the island is only 30,000, and the field restricted, yet much itinerant work is done, and there is a healthy native church. The membership is forty-one, with a Sunday school attendance of forty. Last year $190 was contributed, an average per member of nearly five dollars!

SOUTH AMERICA

South America, so long "the neglected continent," becomes through the opening of the Panama Canal more and more "the continent of opportunity." And the responsibility of the United States to evangelize its sister America becomes correspondingly weighty and urgent.

In Latin America the ALLIANCE has four Missions, namely, in Venezuela, Ecuador, Argentine and Chile, in South America. The greatest enemy of Protestant evangelical missions in Latin America is Rome with her ignorance, superstition and priest-craft. But everywhere the power of Roman Catholicism over the people is weakening. And the future, yes, the *present* menace of spiritual missionary forces are atheism on the one hand and cold formal Christianity on the other hand.

VENEZUELA

The ALLIANCE Mission in Venezuela comprises four stations, three outstations, five missionaries and five native workers.

Our Mission was opened in 1895, Miss White and Miss Lanman being the pioneer missionaries. Two years later Mr. and Mrs.

Bailly reached the field. In 1903 the first native church was organized; while in 1908 our Mission dedicated the first Protestant church in Venezuela. "There are three native churches with sixty-seven members. Last year there were fifteen additions by baptism, and twenty-five were hopefully converted. One hundred children attend the Sunday school classes, and twenty-eight the day schools. There is a training class for native workers, with eight students, four of whom are Porto Ricans. This school is connected with the Industrial Home at Hebron, a few miles from Caracas."

ECUADOR

The ALLIANCE Mission in Ecuador comprises three stations,* three outstations, five missionaries, and two native workers.

Our Mission was opened about 1897, when Mr. and Mrs. Tarbox and Mr. Fritz went to the field. Following them somewhat later were Mr. and Mrs. Crisman and Mr. and Mrs. Polk. Ecuador was once the most deeply sunk of all South American republics, because of the shadow of baptized paganism. Now, however, the country is opening its

---

*Namely, Monte Cristi, Ambato and Quito.

doors to Christ and offering special opportunities for Christian civilization. We have a native church membership of twenty-seven, with a Sunday school enrollment of eighty-five. Last year there were three baptisms and twenty-five inquirers. The religious outlook is bright and encouraging.

ARGENTINE

The ALLIANCE Mission in the Argentine comprises three stations, four outstations, eight missionaries, and two native workers. One of our stations, Gualeguay, is in the northern part of the province of Gualeguay, while the other two stations, Azul and Olivarria, are located not far apart in the western section.

Our Mission was opened in 1897. "The republic of Argentina is the most progressive country in the world, commercially and industrially; but its people are in the darkest moral and spiritual night and sunk in complete indifference and insensibility. The church of Rome has so utterly lost its hold upon the community that not more than ten per cent. of its university students have any faith in Christianity, and, worse still, have forever condemned Christianity because of the exhibition of it which the Roman church has so long afforded. They are, therefore, harder to reach than the heathen."

According to statistics we have a native church membership of 100, with a Sunday school enrollment of 140. Last year there were five baptisms and nearly a hundred inquirers. While the spiritual need of the Argentine is desperate, the missionary outlook is bright and hopeful. Indeed, the forward movement has started in our Mission. A new station, Tapalquè, has been opened through a tent campaign. A gracious revival has visited the place, and already there are twenty believers. These results have encouraged the mission to launch out in an extensive tent work to possess new territory.

CHILE

The ALLIANCE Mission in Chile comprises twelve stations, twenty outstations, ten missionaries, and seventeen native workers.

Our Chile Mission was opened in 1907. In that year the Rev. H. L. Weiss, who with his wife had been working with the Methodists, "heard that there was a colony of German people who had had a revival and were working on independent lines. They had been praying for just such a man, and it did not take long for him to meet them and effect a union, which was immediately sealed by God in the conviction and conversion of souls. Thus the great work of creating the first native church in Chile was accomplished." This was in the city of Valdivia, which contains our strongest native church. It has a membership of 100, and has for years supported its pastor. Valdivia has three outstations, with a number of permanent preaching places manned by eight native pastors. Indeed, only two mission stations are in the hands of foreign missionaries, namely, Santiago and Osomo. All are loyal and successful, souls being saved in every place.

A printing press has been installed and has been greatly blessed in the wide circulation of Gospel tracts. A little steamer, the "Messenger," plies the navigable rivers. Mr. S. W. Diener has entered upon work among the Indians, and has opened a school among them. He is engaged in acquiring the Indian language. Miss Le Fevre hopes soon to open an orphanage. She already has a few happy children under her care, and is teaching them the ways of the Lord. Between our Chilean and Argentine fields, which are separated by the Andes, are a company of believers. Indeed, a string of stations from coast to coast would be entirely practicable, and would aid in solving the problem of evangelizing the Indians of Peru, Bolivia, Brazil, and the Argentine. Until recently very few successful attempts have been made to reach them. Mr. Diener must be assisted and sustained in his heroic work. Who will go?

According to statistics we have a native church membership of 508. Last year $4,-400 was contributed for the Lord's work. There is a strong and flourishing associate work among German colonists, under the leadership of Mr. Barkowitch.

In the above fields there are 43,000,000 dependent upon our ALLIANCE Missions for the Bread of Life.

An average of one missionary to 164,000 heathen.

An average of one native worker to 111,-000 heathen.

An average of one church member to 8,242.

GIVE, PRAY, GO!

CHAPTER VII

RETROSPECT AND PROSPECT

𝕋 WENTY-FIVE years! The quarter centennial of the ALLIANCE is a good point of vantage from which to look backward upon the past and to look forward into the future.

RETROSPECT

As the thoughtful and devout mind reviews the history of the CHRISTIAN AND MISSIONARY ALLIANCE, the words of Balaam, when he gazed upon the camp of Israel spread out before him, rise to the lips:

"What hath God wrought?" (Numbers 23: 23).

But in particular, this brief record of achievements suggests several reflections:

First.—A conviction that the movement is of God. For more than a quarter of a century before its inception, the Lord had chosen and by His providences had been educating and training the founder and leader of the ALLIANCE. Moreover, for many years

and by varied experiences hundreds of lives
throughout this country and Canada, and indeed all over the world, had been Divinely
prepared to embrace heartily and support
loyally the new evangelistic and missionary
movement, launched at Old Orchard in the
summer of 1887. Finally, the time was ripe
in the Christian world. As we have seen, the
impulse of five spiritual movements, taking
their rise in the last century, finds expression
and receives emphasis in our rounded testimony and simple organization: Evangelism,
Holiness, Divine Healing, Foreign Missions,
and the Lord's Return.

Second.—A recognition that the seal of
God has rested upon the movement. No
candid, spiritual person, who knows our history, can escape this. Born in an atmosphere
of faith and prayer, the ALLIANCE grew up
amid an environment of considerable misun-
derstanding and consequent frequent misrep-
resentation. In some quarters, indeed, the
Society has always met antagonism, which is
very largely due either to erroneous views or
inadequate knowledge as to its true spirit and
real purpose. Of course, our teaching on
Divine healing and, to a less degree, on sanc-

tification and the return of the Lord are, because of the nature of the doctrines, opposed by many of the Lord's people. Reproach on account of its position on these vital Scripture truths, the ALLIANCE must expect and may even welcome. But that to so large an extent evangelical churches, multitudes of whose members either are connected with the ALLIANCE or attend its services, and to whose entire membership indeed the ALLIANCE desires to minister the truth and grace committed to it, should continue to reject its message or question its motive, is cause for serious and distressing regret. However, in face of much criticism of its methods and strong opposition to its teachings, the ALLIANCE has reached vigorous manhood, and the pleasure of the Lord has prospered in its hands. But again, through the loving kindness and good providence of God our Society has survived without division or serious loss shocks from within the ranks. Of those numbered among us during the quarter century the words of the Apostle are true of some: "They went out from us, but they were not of us; for if they had been of us they would no doubt have continued with us: but they

went out, that they might be made manifest
that they were not of us" (1 John 2:19).
Of those who "went out from us," some indeed returned. In truth, the Gospel of the
fulness of Jesus for spirit, soul and body is
a searcher of hearts and a weigher of mo-
tives. One cannot preach it or teach it WITH
POWER apart from a vital experience of its
renewing, transforming and energizing influences. And if one be a living exponent of
the Gospel of the fulness of Jesus, he will
be actuated by the unselfish purpose of Him
Who "came not to be ministered unto but to
minister" (Matthew 20:28). But He who
has led will, we believe, still lead and continue to let His approving seal rest upon
our beloved Alliance.

Third.—A spirit of joyous praise for many
truly remarkable achievements. A few statistical items and jottings by the way may be
left to tell their own story.

During the quarter century over $4,000,000
(four million dollars) have been raised for
the varied purposes of our work. Of this
large amount the greater proportion has gone
to the foreign field. When it is recalled that
the constituency of the ALLIANCE is far from

wealthy, that most of the free-will offerings
are for small amounts and that the money
given represents in multiplied instances rigid
economy and in many lives sacrificial suffering, surely this is a marvelous achievement,
which calls forth devout praise.

Throughout the twenty-five years the
Gospel of the fulness of Jesus has been proclaimed to literally hundreds of thousands of
people in many lands and in varied languages,
and just as literally thousands and even tens
of thousands have come unto the experience
of Christ as Saviour, Sanctifier, Healer and
Coming Lord.

In the home land and in the foreign field
the Society owns property valued at more
than half a million ($500,000) dollars.

To our Missions in China have been provi-
dentially given the signal honor of opening
the hostile provinces of Kwang-si and Hunan
and of being the first missionaries to Tibet
and Annam.   Furthermore, our beautiful
new American church in Jerusalem is a notable achievement of Divine goodness.   The
ALLIANCE built the first Protestant church in
Venezuela.

Last year the membership of our native

churches, numbering not far from 6,000, increased thirteen (13) per cent. Here in America the Protestant church membership increased only a little over one (1) per cent. "The native churches have attained a high standard of spiritual life and vigor. Spirit-filled and efficient native workers have been called, trained and sent forth. There have been many wonderful cases of Divine healing in answer to prayer."

Fourth.—A spirit of deep and devout humility. While many worthy achievements of the past stand to its credit, yet the ALLIANCE should not glory therein. Rather, we are sure, does the Society take the place assigned it by the words of our Lord: "So likewise ye, when ye shall have done all these things which are commanded you, say, we are unprofitablbe servants; we have done that which was our duty to do" (Luke 17, 10). Writing of our quarter centennial Dr. R. H. Glover says: "While it is cause for thanksgiving and encouragement, it is no ground for self-content or congratulation, but only an incentive to greater effort and a stepping-stone to larger achievement. The unmet need is appalling, the opportunity in-

spiring, the call imperative. And so the cele-
bration of this anniversary is designed to be
of the nature not of a mere commemoration
of the past, but rather of a greater forward
movement to meet the open doors and reach
the regions beyond."

Fifth.—A spirit of deep appreciation and
profound gratitude. The ALLIANCE has a
long and ever lengthening roll of faithful,
loyal and efficient foreign missionaries and
home workers. This historical sketch is intended to be, not an exploitation of persons
but a narration of providences. The writer
is sure that he is not astray in the belief that
his brethren would prefer to stand, even un-
named, in the background and permit our
adorable Lord and His glorious Gospel to fill
the picture. A nobler, grander, humbler,
more self-sacrificing, and more Christlike
body of men and women than our ALLIANCE
workers at home and abroad it would be
hard to find. Indeed, their like, we believe,
are not upon the earth. Of them, with respect to our honored and beloved leader,
may be said what was written of King Saul:
"There went with him a band of men, whose
hearts God had touched" (1 Samuel 10:26).

But of the missionaries and home workers, who during the quarter century have been called to their eternal rest, the ALLIANCE has a long honor roll. Indeed, it is sadly true, as our president has said, that "after the lapse of almost an entire generation many, if not most, of the original friends and supporters have passed or are passing away." What a rich and precious heritage is left us in the memory of our beloved fellow laborers who are with the Lord."

PROSPECT

Turning to consider the future of the ALLIANCE, all the friends and lovers of the work hope and pray that "the glory of this latter house shall be greater than that of the former" (Haggai 2, 9). There are indeed convincing reasons why it should be so.

First.—The call of God rests upon the Society now in even greater degree than at its inception a quarter of a century ago. By no manner of means has the ALLIANCE outlived its original purpose or Divine usefulness. Far from being in a state of decrepitude, the movement has not yet reached adult maturity. Rather is it throbbing with the full pulses and expanding with the exuberant vitality and strength of youthful manhood. Larger than ever before is the place which the ALLIANCE fills in the religious world. During the twenty-five years of its existence no organization animated by a like spirit or serving a like purpose has sprung up. Both the message and the mission of our Society are unique.

Second.—The message and the mission of the ALLIANCE are as wide as the Gospel and as varied as human need. Salvation from sin, sanctification and satisfaction through Christ, supernatural health for the body, and the blessed hope of the return of the Lord— any one of these vital Scriptural truths alone makes a timely message and constitutes a worthy mission. But "the city lieth foursquare." And in combining and proclaiming the Fourfold Gospel our Society has, we believe, the greatest and grandest Scriptural message of any sectarian church or religious organization upon earth. "The whole Gospel for the whole man and for the whole world." This is at once our special calling and distinctive testimony.

Third.—The entire homeland in its vast

length and breadth *needs* the message and
testimony of the ALLIANCE, and the message
and testimony of the ALLIANCE *must be
given* to the entire homeland in its vast length
and breadth. It is a sound commercial principle that the country-wide markets are open
to a satisfactory commodity of general use.
So our Society has a Gospel for which the
people of the United States and Canada are
spiritually hungry, although for the large
part they may know it not; and when they
hear the glad news of the fulness of Jesus,
multitudes will joyfully receive it.   It is
gratifying to record a growing spirit of
friendliness and even cordiality towards the
ALLIANCE on the part of the pastors and
members of evangelical churches. From the
beginning many of the strongest supporters
of our work have been pastors and members
of evangelical denominations.   Indeed, quite
commonly   our   conventions   are   held   in
churches through the fine courtesy and warm
co-operation of pastors and officiary.

But the time is ripe for a forward movement. The Divine call comes: "Enlarge the
place of thy tent, and let them stretch forth
the curtains of thine habitations; spare not,

lengthen thy cords, and strengthen thy stakes; for thou shalt break forth on every side" (Isaiah 54:2). Where one has hitherto heard the message of the ALLIANCE, there should henceforth be a hundred, a thousand, even tens of thousands. Thus will be created the new and greatly enlarged sustaining constituency, which the Board feels to be imperative, if it is to enter the wide-open doors of emergency and opportunity in mission lands. Of course an advancement means more workers and larger funds. However, for the lack of these the Forward Movement need not halt. Expansion and development may come in the same way the Society sprang up and grew. All over this country and Canada are wide stretches of territory as yet unreached. In these regions every believer in the Fourfold Gospel might become the *nucleus* of a new work in the community where he lives. Individually, here and there, any person who has accepted the truths which the ALLIANCE proclaims, can open his or her home for services. While desirable, a leader is not necessary, especially at the outset. Organize prayer bands, if only of two or three, and let them meet regularly once a week for intercession. Subscribe for THE ALLIANCE WEEKLY, and send to headquarters for our official literature. For a comparatively small sum an order of assorted mottoes, books, and tracts will be sent to any address. Circulate these among your neighbors. *Write at once.* Let every reader into whose life blessing has come through the ALLIANCE ponder prayerfully these two Scriptures: "Lord, what wilt Thou have me to do?" (Acts 9: 6). "Whatsoever He saith unto you, do it" (John 2: 5).

Fourth.—Even more, if anything, than in the homeland the message and ministry of the ALLIANCE are needed in the foreign mission field. The Gospel of the fulness of Jesus finds a ready access to the heathen, their minds and hearts being peculiarly open to the truths of Divine healing and the return of the Lord. Indeed, some of the most remarkable instances of healing in our work have been native Christians and even among unconverted heathen

But the missionary achievements of the ALLIANCE, extensive and glorious as they have been, can be regarded only as a good beginning. In fact, at present the Society

is facing a missionary opportunity unprece-
dented and unparalleled in our history. Dr.
R. H. Glover thus draws the general picture:

"From nearly every ALLIANCE field comes
a loud call for more workers. On some
fields the need is a desperate one. The gaps
made by death and other causes have not
been filled, and the present workers are overtaxed almost to the breaking point. The
growth of the work already in hand calls for
a larger staff to do justice to it. Providential
events and conditions in many lands, most
notably in China, Palestine, the Congo and
South America, have created an opportunity
unparalleled in the history of missions. *The
clock of time is striking the crisis hour of
world-wide evangelization.* Open doors are
on every hand. Multitudes of people have
suddenly become friendly and receptive. The
harvest is on. The present force of workers
is utterly inadequate for the new and thrilling situation. Nor will this opportunity wait,
especially in some lands. It must be promptly
seized or forever lost. *Which is it to be?*

Answering to these conditions and needs
abroad is the fact that recruits are available.
At the present time FIFTY graduates of

ALLIANCE training institutions stand approved by the Board as qualified and desirable missionary candidates. It is to be regretted that only TWELVE of these are MEN, inasmuch as the most urgent need is for this class. Indeed, certain important posts on several fields can only be filled by men. At least five men should be sent at once to each of the three fields of China, as well as to the Congo and South America, three each to Palestine and Annam, and two each to Japan, the Soudan and the Philippines. Women, too, are needed and will be welcome in all the fields.

The very lowest aim should be to raise the number of missionaries to THREE HUNDRED before the end of the anniversary year. Candidates are ready and longing to go, and the Board to send them. What is lacking is money to send and support them. *Who will rise to the need and privilege* and SEND ONE?"

From the comprehensive survey of the president a few striking details of the picture thus so graphically drawn may be given.

Through the recent marvelous changes and transformations in the Turkish empire the entire Moslem world and particularly Palestine centering in and around Jerusalem, is opening to the Gospel. The trans-Jordanic region is turning towards the light, and a railway penetrating the heart of Arabia is unbolting the doors and levelling the barriers of the land of Ishmael.

India is open and white to harvest. The higher classes are crying for the Gospel, and the doors that were closed a dozen years ago are open to-day. Indeed, the Christian community has increased immensely faster than even the population of India.

In China, the land of lightning changes and kaleidoscopic wonders, all the provinces are wide open to the Gospel. The entire country is looking for Western civilization, and if she does not get our Christ, she will get our agnosticism and ungodliness. Officially China recently asked for the prayers of the Christian world. And Dr. Sun Yat Sen, the leader of the revolutionary party, has advised his people to listen to the missionaries, and to believe in their Gospel, because Christianity is the best religion for China to-day.

Tibet has opened its gates. With a small amount of money, along a border line of 400 miles, a dozen cities could be opened, each the center of a population of hundreds of thousands of souls with not a single voice to witness for Jesus Christ.

Annam with its twenty-one millions of people without a single missionary has just opened its doors, and before our little band of pioneers in Touraine a golden opportunity opens, for the fields are white unto harvest.

Japan is at the parting of the ways—godless civilization or a forward movement towards Christianity. The students of the great university of Tokyo, over five thousand in number, have by a vast majority renounced the native religions, and are agnostics, ready to accept God's truth or the devil's lie.

Christianity is fairly sweeping over the Philippine Islands, and with reinforcements and increased funds the archipelago will soon become almost a home mission field.

Our Soudan Mission is facing a crisis. The odds of dangerous climate and Moslem opposition are staggering. But the precious though slight fruit already gathered, the many lonely graves, and above all the intrepid spirit of the little band of workers call for immediate advancement. Extraordinary success attends our Congo Mission, both in the preservation of the lives and health of our missionaries and in the gratifying ingathering of souls. Last year more members were added to the native church than have joined the Gospel Tabernacle in New York in the past ten years!

What can we say of Latin America? Romanism, it is true, has lost its power, but alas! Protestant Christianity has not replaced it. The people of Central and South America, who have renounced the superstition and priestcraft of the Roman church are on the verge of agnosticism, atheism, and utter godlessness. At the same time every door is wide open and the fields are white and ready for the harvest.

Surely, in the heathen world this is the day of our opportunity and emergency. The crisis hour has come of which the Lord spake in 2 Samuel 5:24: "And let it be, when thou hearest the sound of a going in the tops of the mulberry trees, that thou shall bestir thyself; for then shall the Lord go out before thee."

Fifth.—The supreme belief of the founder

and organizer of the ALLIANCE was that the movement would hasten the return of the Lord Jesus. But how much more should this belief inspire all our hearts now, for we are twenty-five years nearer this glorious consummation of the age! Indeed, the great objective of our missionary achievements is the "blessed hope" of the Coming of Christ. For Jesus said: "And this Gospel of the kingdom shall be preached in all the world for a witness unto all the nations; and then shall the end come." Speaking of the missionary opportunity of the ALLIANCE the president says:

"The signs of the soon coming of the Lord Jesus intensify the crisis and the emergency. If the preaching of the Gospel unto all nations as a witness be the one urgent condition whose realization will bring the end, surely no more powerful incentive to world-wide evangelization can appeal to our hearts. At best our work is only apprentice work preliminary and preparatory to His great finishing touch, and how we long for the Master to come and bring that touch and climax to our poor, imperfect attempts at service. They tell of a gifted artist who was struggling to express on canvas the great vision that had

come to his soul, and how at last, discouraged
by his inability to do justice to his own ideal,
he left his painting incomplete and wrote in
his diary a little cry of self-dispair. That
night the old master came in disguise to the
studio, to which he still retained a pass key,
and as he gazed upon the striking outline
upon the canvas and thought of the artist
whose inmost soul he understood so well, he
seemed to enter into his conception, and
seizing the brush he finished the painting as
only he could have done, and quietly stole
away. When the young artist returned to
his studio, he gazed in rapt astonishment
upon his finished work, and bursting into
tears he cried, 'No one but the master himself could have done this.' So some day
Christ our Master will come and finish our
poor 'prentice work with His own glorious
touch, and the things which for twenty centuries the struggling church has been inade-
quately endeavoring to accomplish, will burst
upon the vision of the universe in all the
glory of His finished plan. A nation shall
be born in a day, and the knowledge of the
Lord shall cover the earth as the waters cover
the sea. Oh, if it be true that all the provi-

dence of God can do in fulfilment of prophecy, and all that the Holy Ghost has promised
in the preparation of the bride, if it be true
that these things are in great measure accomplished, and the advent chariots are only
waiting until the last human tribe has heard
the message, and received the invitation to
the marriage of the lamb, surely all this
creates an emergency, a responsibility, a
supreme incentive, sufficient to set our hearts
on fire, to redeem the time, and finish our
great missionary trust before our generation
shall have passed away."

"Surely I come quickly.

Amen; come, Lord Jesus" (Rev. 22:20).

OUR HONORED DEAD

"It was the beautiful thought of the early Church that there were three forms of martyrdom and that every Christian could be a martyr in one or other of these three ways.

"First, a martyr in will but not in deed. Like : t. John, living longest of all the little band of Apostles, and yet always willing and ready to lay his life down when and where the Lord should desire. But in his case 'the will was taken for the deed,' and the long life was ended peacefully by a natural death.

"Second, a martyr in deed but not in will, like the innocent babes of Bethlehem, dying as children for the Lord Jesus without knowing it.

"Third, a martyr in deed and in will like St. Stephen, facing death in the fulness of his manhood, and freely giving his life to and for Jesus, his Life-Giver.

"It is interesting to notice that we have all three of these forms of martyrdom illustrated in the record of the departed missionaries of the Christian and Missionary Alliance."

These words taken from the memorial paper of the late Dr. Henry Wilson, read before our Annual Council in May, 1901, may fittingly stand at the head of this roll of our honored dead.

The purpose of this memorial chapter is to record the names of all our missionaries who have died during the quarter-century. Moreover, the attempt has been made to give some facts concerning every precious life that has been laid down for Christ's sake. Furthermore, there has been added a brief appreciation of a few of our more prominent leaders and supporters in the homeland.

India

HELEN DAWLLY

Helen Dawlly had the honor of being the first Alliance missionary regularly appointed to India, and in keeping with this distinction she was a woman of heroic mould. When she sailed for India, she had money to take her only to Liverpool, but her trunk was labelled "Bombay." At Poona she established a school for Eurasian children, which is still sustained on the original lines of faith and trust in God. Miss Dawlly died in the midst of her great work at Poona, in February, 1893. Her character was strong, her memory is fragrant.

Mr. and Mrs. J. E. Bendixon.

This Godly couple was the gift of Sweden to the Alliance. It is recalled that Mrs. Bendixon in spite of difficulties made fine progress with the language, while Mr. Bendixon had a rarely sweet and victorious spirit. Their deaths marked the first break in the ranks of our India missionaries; the wife passing away in February, 1895, and the husband a few weeks later.

Annie Bush

In Annie Bush strength and winsomeness were blended. She died in March, 1895, and is buried in the graveyard where rest the remains of Bishop Heber.

Rev. James Foster

Mr. Foster is remembered as a particularly bright and happy Christian. He died at Khamgaon, in March, 1895.

Dr. Court T. Simmons

This Scotch physician, after being healed, gave up his practice in Denver, Colorado, and went to India full of zeal and faith. It is said that while he prayed, heathen turned their idols to the wall. He contracted blood poisoning in one of our orphanages, ministering to a young native, and died in June, 1895.

Daniel McDonald

This man was a fine product of Canadian ruggedness and consecration. He had been on the field only a few months, when he died in August, 1895.

Mrs. Effie Holmes Wood

There is abundant testimony to the loveableness of this young woman, whose life was marked by rare consecration and singular devotion to God. She died in October, 1895, at Buldana.

Donald Herron

Donald Herron was a big man physically and spiritually. His itinerating tours developed fine evangelistic gifts. He died from a sunstroke in January, 1896.

Malcolm Moss

Malcolm Moss joined the Alliance after reaching India. While pioneering with a view of entering Assam, he contracted smallpox and died in February, 1896.

Mrs. Emma Royle Bannister

England was the native land of this splendid woman who with few advantages and amid many difficulties acquired a firm mastery of the language. She bravely endured the hardships of early Gospel touring, sleeping many a night in the ox-cart. Mrs. Bannister died in March, 1896.

Sarah J. Montgomery

Than this faithful woman a nobler spirit never left the Institute for the mission field. In July, 1896, she had a triumphant death, singing in her closing moments:

> "Arms of Jesus, fold me closer;
> Closer to Thy loving breast."

Mrs. Priscilla Burgess Guttridge

Mrs. Guttridge went to India in 1888 in Salvation Army work, joining the Alliance in 1892. Uprightness, sincerity and endurance were her chief traits. She died in England in the fall of 1896.

Mary Olmstead

Miss Olmstead was one of our ablest India missionaries. She was a graduate of Vassar College and for years a successful teacher. Her influence over the native Christians was exceptional and touching. She died from cholera in the spring of 1897. An old man asked the privilege of driving the ox-cart carrying her body to the grave, exclaiming: "Oh, how she loved us." It is said of her that she knew how to yield and give honor to others.

REV. M. I. GARRISON

This humble and holy man was in middle life when he went to India, but had a missionary career of singular wisdom and efficiency. His work abides, being carried on indeed by his two sons who are also India missionaries: Rev. Alle I. and Rev. Kiel D. Garrison. Mr. Garrison died from consumption in April, 1897. "The night before he passed away he received from the Master a distinct conviction that he was about to go home. The next day he called his family around him and left the most minute directions and particulars in all respects, and then in the spirit of tranquil and triumphant faith he fell asleep in his Master's arms."

MRS. DONALD HERRON

After her husband's death Mrs. Herron labored faithfully for fifteen months in the difficult field of Jalgaon. She was a great sufferer from asthma, dying in April, 1897.

Mrs. George Carroll

Mrs. Carroll went to India under the Pentecost Band, afterwards joining the Alliance. She died from consumption in Bombay, in January, 1898.

Miss M. D. Fecke

Miss Fecke had been matron in a German Hospital in Chicago. After about three years in India she died from Typhoid fever, in December, 1899. She was known as a woman of sound judgment, while discretion marked all her ways.

Kate Parks

Miss Parks went to India in 1894, confining her work to Bombay, where in Berachah Home she ministered faithfully to all who came for rest and help. She was specially interested in the Jews of the city. No missionary in sickness or in need had a kinder friend than she. Miss Parks died from smallpox in February, 1900.

Emma Smyley

Emma Smyley went to India in 1894, devoting her life to the Kaira Orphanage. During the famine season she overworked and her health gave way. While resting in Bombay, expecting soon to sail for America, she passed away in June, 1900. Unselfish devotion to the Master and His service characterized her life.

Mrs. Annie Armstrong Back

Mrs. Back died on the field in February, 1901. She overtaxed herself during the famine season. She is remembered as a modest, gentle, winsome woman, devoted to the Lord and to her work.

Rev. C. C. and Mrs. Lenth

This consecrated and well equipped couple went to India in 1894. Besides considerable touring they devoted themselves to famine relief work. At one time they had 1,800 natives under their care. Mr. Lenth died from exposure to the sun and fever in August, 1901, Mrs. Lenth following him a few months later. The husband was an enthusiastic, self-sacrificing worker, while the wife was richly developed in the graces of the Holy Spirit, giving herself first unto the Lord and then unreservedly to the work He gave her to do.

Rev. Gideon W. Woodward

With an excellent scientific training Mr. Woodward went to India in 1894. In Gujerat he gave himself unstintedly to famine relief work, contracting a fever which ended his useful life in the summer of 1901. Mr. Woodward was an excellent example of a business man and a preacher of the Gospel. He became a successful soul winner. He was a man of saintly spirit and rare devotion to the Master.

Mrs Hattie Mallory Fuller

Hattie Mallory was the daughter of the Rev. O. E. Mallory, D.D., an honorary vice-president of the Alliance and one of the oldest and staunchest supporters of the movement. She went to India in 1894, returning on furlough in 1901 to visit her invalid mother, who soon afterwards passed away. She had a fruitful ministry among the women of Bombay. In September, 1902, Miss Mallory became the wife of the Rev. M. B. Fuller, superintendent of our mission in India, but two months later died from malarial fever. "A marked characteristic in her life was cheerfulness, especially in meeting trials and difficulties. She always looked up and saw a way through. In this she was an inspiration to many lives. Her faith in God was the kind that risked her all upon Him. Her walk with

God and man was marked by an open, free spirit. There was nothing hid."

Mrs Lida Allen Phelps

Lida Allen was well educated and before attending the Institute in New York, during the session of 1896-'97, she had taught school and been an officer in the Loyal Temperance Legion, "laboring faithfully to train young minds against alcohol and narcotics." She had a sweet, kind and patient spirit. Through an act of kindness to a native she contracted smallpox from which she died, in October, 1903.

Rev. T. Elmer Dutton

Mr. Dutton had a strong, brave, enduring personality. Moreover, he had varied gifts, among others marked musical ability. Mr. Dutton was sent to India in 1892, and had a splendid record of thorough, enduring work. He died from smallpox in 1903.

Ellen C. Decker

In her home town Ellen Decker had a fine preparation for her service in India, being active in Christian work and ministering especially to the sick and destitute. On the field during her one year of service it was said that she lived more than most do in many years. Miss Decker was a woman of well balanced, deeply spiritual and intensely practical character. She died in November, 1903.

MRS. SEARLE

Mrs. Searle was a noble, Godly woman. She was one of our best missionaries. As much as any martyr she laid down her consecrated, self-sacrificing life in November, 1905.

REV. CARL ERICSON

Carl Ericson was a Swede, educated at Colgate College, and an ordained Baptist minister. He went to India in 1892, his missionary career being marked by indefatigable zeal and spiritual fervor. He had evangelistic gifts, and was one of our strongest and most successful missionaries. He died from fever in December, 1906. As he was passing away the missionaries around his bedside sang:

"I saw him overcoming through all the swelling strife,
Until he crossed the threshold of God's eternal life;
The crown, the throne. the scepter, the name, the stone so white,
Were his who found in Jesus the yoke and burden light."

REV. PETER C. MOODY

Peter Moody was a remarkable man and a

remarkable missionary. He gave his life to India because of a marked experience of physical healing. While at Poona holding services in the Taylor High School he contracted fever from the effects of which he died, in December, 1906. As he was dying he turned to those who were kneeling beside his bed and whispered, "Yes, Lord." Of him it may be said that he was filled with faith and the Holy Ghost.

Mrs. Maude Weist Turnbull

Maude Weist came of a prominent and Godly family, her father, S. L. Weist, of Harrisburg, Pennsylvania, being publisher of the United Evangelical Church. She went to India in 1902, her marriage a few years later involving a change of field and the acquiring of a new language. Mrs. Turnbull had a sweet, hopeful, winsome spirit, keen mental ability, steady perseverance and a well balanced judgment. For a number of years she was editor of the "India Alliance." Her death occurred in November, 1909.

Alice Yoder

Looming large among our India missionaries is the name of Alice Yoder. She was one of the best products of the Pennsylvania

Germans. She died in October, 1908. "She was a woman of remarkable strength of character, of unusual versatility of practical gifts, and yet of utmost consecration of spirit. Hence she was qualified for great and varied responsibilities, and she met them bravely and discharged them efficiently. She was in charge of the large orphanage at Khamgaon. There she had large scope for her varied and unusual gifts, natural and spiritual. In one of her last letters she wrote: 'I am working as if I were to remain here always, and I live as if I might be called to leave it at any time.' Of Alice Yoder one of her associates said, 'Every place that she occupied she filled full.' "

Mrs. Carrie Bates Rogers

Carrie Bates was the daughter of a Baptist minister, and when a young girl experienced a remarkable healing and received a clear call to the mission field. She fell asleep in Jesus in January, 1909. "The name of Carrie B. Bates heads the list on the Record Book of the Indian Mission of the Christian and Missionary Alliance. She was every inch a missionary. From early life she had known great bodily weakness, and her heroic life involved such hardships as to weigh her last days with constant suffering. Just as the end approached, although she had been unconscious for thirty-six hours, she lifted up her eyes and gazed steadfastly and intently on some invisible object, and so taken up with heavenly rapture she forgot to take another breath and fell asleep in Jesus without a struggle. Her prayer-life was strong, her devotion to her work intense."

LUCY HOLMES

Lucy Holmes was of sturdy New England stock and for twenty-five years was a teacher in Mount Holyoke Seminary. She offered herself for India in 1894 and was a staunch believing in the fourfold Gospel, finding inspiration and joy in the blessed hope of the return of the Lord. Indeed, sne radiated good cheer wherever she went. At the age of seventy-four she died from fever in 1913.

HATTIE O'DONNELL

Canada gave Hattie O'Donnell to India, whither she sailed on short notice, not being given time to say "Good-bye" to her parents. This shows the stuff she was made of. Like Caleb of old "she wholly followed the Lord."

She was a true shepherd to her India converts. Miss O'Donnell died in the fall of 1913.

China
Rev. William Cassidy

This minister and physician was our pioneer missionary to China. In the providence of God, however, he was not permitted to enter the country, contracting smallpox through having taken steerage passage on a Pacific steamer and dying in Kobe, Japan, in 1889. In every way William Cassidy was preeminently strong in his consecration to Christ and his devotion to the cause of missions.

Mrs. Susie Beals

Mrs. Beals went to the foreign field from the home work of the Alliance, her husband having had charge for some time of our publishing interests. She had a very brief missionary career, reaching China in March and dying in October, 1892. She had a sweet, patient spirit, and was a great sufferer.

Rev. W. I. Knapp

Mr. Knapp had a short term of service. Indeed, he had but recently acquired the language, being of great usefulness in making preparation for new missionaries, when he died in May, 1892.

J. H. HODGES

Mr. Hodges was connected with our Central China Mission. He was very successful with the language, and was possessed with a winning spirit, courageous faith, and a single-hearted devotion to God. He died from smallpox in March, 1894.

REV. C. H. REEVES

Mr. Reeves was one of our first workers and earliest superintendents in South China. From the first, he cherished the boldest and most far-reaching plans for the evangelization of Kwang Si. He had been on the field only about six years when he died from smallpox contracted in an interior town, in March, 1898. Mr. Reeves' life was a rare blend of strength and sweetness. He finely exemplified the Christ life.

AGNES COONEY

Miss Cooney died in August, 1900, after three and a half years' service on the South China field. At the time, the whole mission staff was in attendance upon the Annual Conference at Macao, and all knelt at her bedside

renewing their consecration vows. Her marked
devotion to God and intense love for souls
were an inspiration to her fellow workers.
Miss Cooney had an unusually sweet and
strong character.

Mrs. Isaac Hess

Mrs. Hess had a frail body, but a delicate
and refined spirit. She was a true gentle-
woman. "No severer loss could have over-
taken our South China Mission. Her work in
this country before she went to the field and
her beautiful life and multiplied labors in
China made her very dear to all who knew
her."

Theodora Campbell

Miss Campbell went to the field in her maturity and was for some time principal of a
woman's training school in South China. She
not only gave her life, but consecrated her
money to the foreign work. She was a woman
of rare discernment and excellent judgment,
and was one of our strongest and most valuable workers. She died in November, 1905.

Beulah Funk

Beulah Funk came from a consecrated and
Godly family, her father and two brothers

being ministers. She had a nature rarely endowed with the graces of the Spirit. She made a profound impression as a student in the Institute, being a bright and shining light, and exerted a powerful influence among the students. She had four years of fruitful labor in South China, dying in the fall of 1907.

GEORGE SHERMAN

Mr. Sherman was one of the most promising missionary candidates that ever went to the field from our Institute. Along with a thoroughly consecrated spirit, he possessed much practical skill and was of great usefulness on the field. He had just been married a few days when he died from smallpox in the fall of 1907.

EFFIE GREGG

To those who knew her, the name of Effie Gregg was as one among a thousand. She was a unique character, and her consecration and devotion to God were marked. She did a great work in Western China near the borders of Tibet. Her death from smallpox in the Spring of 1908 was peculiarly sad, because she was just in the midst of reaping a gracious harvest for which there had been years of seed sowing.

Mrs. Ruth Lindberg Baer

Both in life and in death, the names of
Effie Gregg and Ruth Lindberg Baer are
linked together. They had been great friends
in the homeland, and stood together on the
foreign field. Indeed, Mrs. Baer contracted
smallpox, from the effects of which she died,
while nursing Miss Gregg through her fatal
illness. Mrs. Baer was a strong, sweet woman,
and her memory is fragrant.

Richard Anderson

Mr. Anderson was one of our earliest missionaries to the Orient, his special field being
Malaysia. He accompanied Mr. Le Lacheur
on one of his tours in the East. He died in
1892 at Singapore.

Rev. Henry Zehr

Mr. Zehr was the best type of a consecrated
and Spirit-filled German missionary. He was
an ordained minister, and had been connected
with the Church Missionary Association. He
was a strong, noble, zealous, devoted soldier
of the cross. He died on the field from smallpox in April, 1904.

Mrs. Ada Beeson Farmer

In March, 1911, Mrs. Farmer fell asleep in

Jesus. She was a member of a well-known family in Mississippi and had been in China for about nine years. She had an intense love for the Lord and His work, great faith in God, unusual executive ability and fidelity to trust and duty. She lived a joyful and victorious life. "Her constant rejoinder to every treaty to spare herself in her toilsome labors was, 'No, I must be true to God and the trust He has given me.'"

Mrs. M. C. Allward

Mrs. Allward was a Canadian, and before coming to the Institute had passed through a severe trial in the death of her husband, who had been an invalid for years. She was a mature Christian, and was gifted in many practical ways. "She was a woman of intense conviction, undying loyalty to her Lord and great boldness in dealing with others as to their obligations to Christ and the world." Mrs. Allward died from smallpox in the spring of 1911.

Rev. G. Lloyd Hughes

Through a providential meeting with an Anamese who was hungry for the Gospel but with whom he could not converse on account

of the barrier of language, Mr. Hughes prayed
and waited for years for an opening to the
22,000,000 unevangelized of Annam. Just
when prayer seemed about to be answered in
his own entry into that land, he sank from
heart disease in Hongkong in the summer of
1911. "He was a man of fervent zeal and
deep consecration and in the very maturity
of his strength and usefulness."

REV. DAVID P. EKVALL

Mr. Ekvall was born in Sweden but educated in this country. He was converted in
early life and after one year at the Institute
went to the field in 1894. He achieved high
attainments in the Chinese language and classics. His work was in part pioneering and in
part literary. He established a Bible Training School for native workers. He died from
typhus fever in May, 1912.

NELLIE S. BOWEN

The latest death on our mission fields is
that of Nellie Bowen, who died of smallpox in Chi Kong, Central China, February
25, 1914. She came from Union City, Ten-
nessee, and was on the field a little over
four years. Miss Bowen had an excellent
educational equipment for her work and

had the heart of a true missionary. She had a gracious, winsome spirit and was "faithful unto death." Nine days before her home-going she said, "There is nothing out of the reach of prayer except that which is out of the will of God."

ELIZABETH FARR BROWN

Elizabeth Farr Brown, the wife of Frank Brown, was a missionary in China for several years. Several children were born to them, but the family were compelled to return home owing to the ill health of Mrs. Brown. Her death, occurring one or two years later, in a western state, was due to tuberculosis. Mrs. Brown was greatly beloved by a wide circle of friends in New York, China, and elsewhere.

Swedish Missionaries

For a number of years the Alliance had a work in the province of Shansi carried on by Swedish missionaries. During the Boxer uprising of 1900 nineteen of these faithful men and women and nearly as many children were massacred. The story has been interestingly and dramatically written by Mrs. K. C. Woodberry, in a volume entitled "Through Blood

Stained Shansi." We here record the names of these honored dead:

Mr. and Mrs. Emil Olsen and three children.

Mr. and Mrs. O. Forsberg and one child.

Mr. and Mrs. C. Blomberg and one or two children.

Mr. and Mrs. W. Noren and two children.

Mr. and Mrs. E. Andersen.

Mr. A. E. Palm.

Miss E. Ericksen.

Mr. and Mrs. O. Bingmark and one or two children.

Mr. and Mrs. M. Nystrom and children.

Mr. and Mrs. C. L. Lundberg and two children.

Miss Gustafsen.

Rev. Emmanuel Olsen

Mr. Olsen was the son of a distinguished Swedish statesman. He was reared in comfort and received a fine education. On long pioneer tours he cheerfully endured severe hardships. He had great faith in God. He organized wide evangelistic work in North Shansi. Mr. Olsen died from pneumonia at Tien Tsin, in January, 1894.

South America
Charles Deming

Mr. Deming belonged to our Venezuela Mission. He was a consistent Christian and a beloved brother in the Lord, and is described as "a model missionary." He died late in 1902.

Irving W. Hathaway

Mr. Hathaway received his education at Northfield Seminary. His plan for a collegiate course was interrupted by God's call to Argentine, South America. He was a sweet Christian brother, well fitted by nature and by grace for his work. He died in Buenos Ayres.

Miss Bechler

Miss Bechler, of our Chile Mission, died of smallpox during the holiday season, 1911. She went to the field from Kansas as an independent worker. She exemplified the best type of German piety, and her quiet, faithful ministry has been greatly missed.

Palestine
James R. Cruickshank

Mr. Cruickshank was the gift of Scotland to our Alliance work. After laboring successfully among the Jews in New York City, he prepared himself for Palestine in our Missionary Training Institute. His career on the field was short, but very successful. He died suddenly in October, 1894. "He was most rigid with himself in matters of conscience, consistency and loyalty to God and to the brethren, and dealt very faithfully with any one of God's children where he saw a compromising disposition with anything that was not clearly from God."

Eliza J. Robertson

Miss Robertson was one of the pioneer missionaries of the Alliance to Palestine, having been a member of the Gospel Tabernacle at New York. She was in mature life when she went to the field, having been thoroughly trained not only along educational lines but also in the discipline of self-denial and hardship. She did a remarkable work in Jerusalem, and together with Miss Lucy Dunn was once spoken of as the woman "who lived next door to God." Her hold among the natives was wonderful, and her work still abides, her memory being a precious legacy to our mission. She passed away in the fall of 1894.

BESSIE KAUFFMAN

Miss Kauffman was a converted and consecrated Jewess who prepared for work in Palestine at our Missionary Training Institute. She had a remarkably strong Christian character, and manifested deep sympathy and ardent love for the people. She went to the field in 1904, and died from cancer while home on furlough, in March, 1907.

MR. AND MRS. GEORGE A. MURRAY

For a number of years, this rugged and Godly couple were connected with our mission in Palestine and did splendid work in Hebron. Mr. Murray was afflicted with lameness, while Mrs. Murray was blind; but despite these serious handicaps, they did much to stir our people in the homeland with interest in missions, and also suffered much hardship and accomplished great good in Palestine. Both passed away quite recently while on furlough.

Africa
Sudan
FRANK M. GATES

W. J. HARRIS

CHARLES HELMICK

MRS. E. KINGMAN

JEAN DICK

These five pioneer missionaries were on the field before the Alliance took over the Sudan Mission. They were the product of a Bible Conference which Dr. H. G. Guinness held in the Middle West in the summer of 1889 in connection with the Y. M. C. A. Mr. Harris, Mr. Gates, and Mrs. Kingman died in July, 1890, Mr. Helmick in October, 1890, and Miss Dick in January, 1891.

Mr. and Mrs. J. W. Meckley

This consecrated, Godly couple went to the field in 1892, but had a very brief missionary career, dying in 1893. In fact, they died the same night, and are buried in the same grave at Magbele.

J. A. Taylor

This devoted missionary sailed for the Sudan in November, 1892, and died in March, 1893. He was a consecrated, self-sacrificing man, and his lonely grave makes a strong plea for the appalling needs of the "Dark Sudan."

Mrs. Roy Codding

Mrs. Codding was a woman of rare Christian spirit, and made a record of faithful service and loving sacrifice on the field. She died while on furlough in Lincoln, Nebraska, in 1894.

D. C. MILLER

Mr. Miller sailed for Africa in December, 1892, and died from smallpox in November, 1894. He had a loving, cheerful disposition and was eminently fitted for missionary work.

G. F. LEGER

Facts concerning Mr. Leger are not available, except that he sailed for the Sudan in December, 1892, and died in May, 1895. He is buried at Tubabudugo. We praise God for this life which was so willingly yielded to His service.

MR. AND MRS. BENJAMIN LUSCOMB

Mr. and Mrs. Luscomb sailed in January, 1895, and died in October of the same year. Mr. Luscomb was a strong Christian character, and had rare evangelistic gifts. It is said of him that he spoke no ill, nor would he listen to any evil report concerning anyone. Mrs. Luscomb had a brief, calm and even life and a glorious death. Her last letter to the homeland closed with the words,

"Yours in patient hope 'til He come."

FIDELIA DREW

Miss Drew sailed in January, 1895, and died three months later. In the homeland, she had been a professional nurse, and was well equipped for missionary work. Her consecration was deep, her courage undaunted, and her faith unwavering.

Mrs. W. E. Shoobridge

This noble, courageous woman came from a missionary family, her brother, the Rev. J. Hal Smith, having been for years connected with our Sudan Mission. Mrs. Shoobridge died in May, 1899, at Makomp.

W. C. Walker

"Mr. Walker was faithful in all his mission work, and his labors were rewarded by the conversion of three of his station men, who bear this blessed testimony: That no one who visited the station was ever allowed to leave without hearing the Gospel."

Alvin Wendell

Mr. Wendell was a man of great faith and courage. In a letter home he wrote, "Many times I would get discouraged were it not for the promise of God, 'My Word shall not return unto Me void.'" He was an indefatigable worker. He died in May, 1897.

Mrs. Minnie May Francis

Mrs. Francis sailed for the Sudan in Janu-

ary, 1897, and died in April of the same year.
Her home-going was particularly sad.
She was rarely developed spiritually, and
finely exemplified the Christ life. Her
death was sanctified by the Lord in the
conversion of several members of her family.

MALEN R. HILL

Malen Hill sailed for the Sudan in January, 1897, and died in April of the same
year. He was buried at Makomp. This
rare young man came from Boone, Ia.,
and attended the Missionary Institute in
New York during the winter of 1894-95.
From there he went to Boydton, Va.,
where his labors among the colored people
were greatly blessed. Mr. Hill is remembered as a man of sweet spirit, who diffused the fragrance of Christ's presence
wherever he went.

MRS. LEONORA BRADSHAW SMITH

Leonora Bradshaw was one of the finest
products of Canada. Before coming to the
Institute in New York in the Fall of '96,
she had taken a hospital course and graduated as a trained nurse. She was a strong
Christian character and leader among the

students. She sailed for the Sudan in '98, and died the following year while en route to the homeland. She was buried in Liverpool.

ELIZABETH GASTON

After receiving a distinct call to the Sudan, Miss Gaston was kept waiting a number of years before reaching the field. She lived, however, only a few months, passing away in 1898. She is remembered as a woman of mental strength and moral determination—"every inch a lady," as someone has described her.

F. E. SWENSON

Mr. Swenson was a sweet, well-educated and a noble Christian gentleman. After a faithful ministry, he went to his reward in 1898.

MERTEN BENTON

Merten Benton sailed for the field in April, 1898, and went home to be with the Lord in 1901. His life was characterized by earnest zeal and devout consecration. He contracted fever while conveying a sick captain from the far station of Tubabudugo to Makomp. A fellow-worker describes him as the most unselfish Christian he ever met.

WILLIAM LEWIS

Mr. Benton and Mr. Lewis were fellow students at the Institute, and went to the Sudan together. Our brother was born in Wales, and was a man of rigid strength and devoutness of spirit. His death was a translation. For two hours before he passed away, heaven seemed opened to his enraptured gaze, and the radiant smile that lighted up his face lingered until his burial. It is said that during his last illness he called for several of the natives to be brought to his room that he might speak to them concerning the Lord Jesus.

TILLIE PATTERSON

Miss Patterson died in November, 1901, shortly after her arrival on the field. She is remembered as a young woman of marked unselfishness and rare devotion.

A. LINCOLN JONES

Mr. Jones was a quiet, humble man, whose going to the field meant a sacrifice of home and business. His life was thoroughly consecrated. He passed to his reward in March, 1904.

ALIDA WELLS

Alida Wells was a young woman of marked strength of personality. She was well educated, truly cultured, and before coming to the Institute, had taught school for a few years. Seldom has one of our students gone to the foreign field better equipped in every way than Alida Wells. She had been on the field only a few weeks when she was called home to be with the Lord in June, 1904.

KATHERINE GEETH

Katherine Geeth and Alida Wells, like David and Jonathan, were together in life, and in death they were not divided. They went to the Sudan at the same time, and died only one day apart. Miss Geeth had been a Christian worker in the homeland, and her ministry had been greatly blessed. She was a strong, reliant, and yet rarely sweet devoted young woman.

GIDEON DICKINSON

Gideon Dickinson went to the field in April, 1904, and died from smallpox in April, 1906. He had a glorious homegoing, which tempered the sad event for his family and friends. He was a quiet, unassuming man who won the love and respect of all. In his diary under date of November 21, 1902, is this entry: "Ceased my struggling. Gave myself to the Holy Spirit to be used or set aside, to be anything or nothing, as he may choose." This, indeed, was the key to our beloved brother's life.

DAVID MUIR

Mr. Muir came from our Alliance work in Avoca, Pennsylvania. He was educated at Northfield. He went to the field in 1904 and died from Blackwater fever, in the summer of 1908. He was a man of deep piety, singular devotion to God and a splendid worker.

Congo

JOHN CONDIT

John Condit was a member of the pioneer party to the Congo in the fall of 1884. His name, indeed, heads the list of our African missionaries. He went to his reward in 1885. While in Westminster Abbey looking at the grave of Livingston, he was heard to say, "Yes, God buries his workmen, but carries out his work. Livingston has passed away, but the work continues, and God is calling out others to fill the places of those who have laid down their lives in the Dark Continent."

Mrs. M. H. Reed

Mrs. Reed was the wife of our first Superintendent of the Congo Mission. She sailed with her husband in the autumn of 1888, and died in the summer of 1890. Mrs. Reed suffered great hardship, and is remembered for her strong faith and trust in God.

John Scott

The names of John and Peter Scott, two brothers, stand high in the record of our Congo Mission. They were Scotch young men, and came from a very Godly family. John Scott was a man of devout spirit and deep consecration. He was one of the first to fall among our early missionaries, in March, 1892.

Clara Stromberg

Clara Stromberg was a bright, talented, beautiful, Swedish girl. Her farewell at the Gospel Tabernacle in May, 1892, was a memorable scene to all who were present. By testimony and song she witnessed for Christ with a face radiant with the light of heaven. She was called home, after being only a few weeks on the field, in July, 1892. In her Bible, she wrote, "Born once in Sweden; born again in Providence. Meet me in the air with Jesus from the Sudan when He comes."

MARY WASHBURN

Miss Washburn sailed for the Congo in May, 1892, and died in July of the same year. She met with a serious accident which developed into the fatal African fever. Her life was wholly devoted to God, and she exerted a strong influence during her brief period of service.

MR. AND MRS. JENNINGS FALCON

Of this Godly couple, it may be said that they were pleasant and beautiful in their lives and in their death they were not divided. Mr. Falcon was a child of the Gospel Tabernacle of New York. He dropped dead suddenly while running across the compound at Vungu, in February, 1893, and Mrs. Falcon did not long survive her husband. There is abundant testimony to the bravery, patience and sweetness of this young life.

FRED CALDERACK

Mr. Calderack sailed for the Congo in

May, 1892, and died the following year. Strength, energy and devotion were the keynotes of his life.

Miss M. Jameison

Miss Jameison went to the field from New England in May, 1892, and gave her life as a sacrifice in the fall of the year. "How beautiful are the feet of them that preach the Gospel of peace and bring glad tidings of good things" (Rom. 10:15).

Albert Horn

Albert Horn went to his reward in 1893. He was a beloved and trusted brother, and his memory deserves to be cherished as one of the immortal names who have given their lives for Africa.

Ardella Riggs

May, 1892, was the year that Miss Riggs went to the field, and 1894 was the year of her death. She is remembered as a lovely, gifted girl, well-known in the homeland, and deeply mourned by the missionary band in Africa.

Harriett Richardson

Miss Richardson died at Vungu early in 1895. "She was a woman of strong faith and deep spiritual character, and during her short life on the field was made a great blessing to her fellow-workers."

WILLIAM WALSH

This good and noble man died at Boma, in 1895, laying down his life willingly as a sacrifice for Africa.

FRED JORGENSON

This noble Swede was a large man, both physically and spiritually. He yielded up his life in the summer of 1895. "He did every task, whether small or great, as unto the Lord. No work was too common to be done faithfully and cheerfully."

ANNETTE WILSON

Miss Wilson died soon after reaching the Congo, in July, 1895. "Strong and true" describes her character. She had been a school teacher, and was somewhat gifted with her pen. It is recalled that she had a remarkable spiritual discernment, and a strong and quick sense of humor.

FRANK AVERY

Mr. Avery sailed for the field in May, 1896, and lived only a few weeks. He is remembered as a quiet, humble, devoted man.

LOUISE COLLINS

Miss Collins sailed in May, 1896, and lived only a short time after reaching the field.   She had been active in Christian work in the Baptist Church in Greenpoint, Brooklyn. She was a lovely character, with a sweet, mild disposition.   Before leaving the homeland, she told her mother not to trouble herself if she should have a grave in Africa, as this would be the most blessed thing that could happen to her.   Her short life made a most profound impression upon the natives, who built a wall around her grave and almost worshiped it.

WILLIAM MACOMBER

Mr. Macomber was a man of rare spiritual character and exceptional gifts.   He sang the Gospel with great power, and wrote a number of hymns, particularly on the subject of the Lord's Return.   While returning home sick on furlough, he died and was buried at Lisbon, Portugal.   Of him it may be said, "He being dead yet speaketh."

MRS. ANNIE SYMINGTON

Mrs. Symington was from the Gospel Tabernacle in New York, and was a woman

of beautiful spirit, and strong and courageous faith. She died at sea, while returning
from the Congo in the spring of 1897, and
was buried in the Canary Islands.

JOHN BULLERKIST

John Bullerkist had been a German ship
carpenter, and did perhaps more than anyone else in building new stations on the
field. The circumstances of his death in
1898 were pathetic. "He had toiled long
and hard, and was very tired. He wrote to
the Board for permission to come home for
a rest, and before the answer came was
taken sick. His testimony was always
clear."

ALFRED P. WOODCOCK

Mr. Woodcock was a remarkable trophy
of grace. For a time, he was Acting Superintendent of our Congo Mission and was in
every way a strong man, loved and trusted
by the missionaries. His death in 1898 was
due to his fidelity to the work. His appeals
for missions in the homeland can never be
forgotten. In his last address, speaking to
young men, he said: "Dear fellows, I want
to say to you. all things are now ready;
come over and help us. But before you

come, consider these things: (1) know God; (2) know of a surety that God wants you in Congo land; (3) brass and courage, or, as Mr. Meritt calls it, stickability, are required; (4) soldiers are needed,—all cannot be commanders or captains."

Hugo P. Schielde

Mr. Schelde sailed in May, 1896, and died the following year. He was an intensely spiritual man. In one of his last letters, he wrote, "I see that a good missionary ought to be a walking encyclopedia. Please pray that I may be kept simple, humble and patient."

Ernest Biber

Ernest Biber was born in Switzerland but educated in this country. Before going to the Congo he was engaged in tent work with Rev. J. E. Ramseyer. He had a gift of illustrating spiritual truth with a crayon. Though but a few months on the field he won the hearts of the natives. He died from sunstroke in November, 1890.

William Wallbrook

Mr. Wallbrook went to the field in the spring of 1895, and died in the homeland in February, 1899. He was a choice spirit, and was a man of high ideals. At the time of his death, he was pastor of the Gospel Church in College Point, N. Y. As a tribute to his memory, a little book of poems and extracts from his diary has been published. He exerted a strong influence in winning men to Christ and in promoting the deepest spiritual life among his fellow-laborers.

Mrs. Louise Muick Gardner

Mrs. Gardner died in the Congo in 1898. "She had a small body and was a marvel of endurance, and always was quiet and sweet."

Mrs. Broome P. Smith

Mrs. Smith died in 1898, after being only a few weeks on the field. "She had a blessed ministry among the Coast people at Boma. Her character and work were a great benediction to the mission."

Mrs. Stevenson

This woman, the first wife of Alva Stevenson, sailed for Congo in the spring of 1896. After furlough she returned with true bravery, leaving her baby in this country. She was a faithful woman, humble and quiet in spirit.

Mrs. Annie C. McDonald

Mrs. McDonald went to the Congo in 1894, and was called home in June, 1909. "She was dauntless, as was proven when six weeks after landing there, she became a widow, but instead of retreating into seclusion, she illustrated to the heathen the consolations of Christ and strengthened her brethren, whom she might justly have left to bear the greater burden of the battle."

Lucy Villars

Miss Villars went to her eternal rest from the Congo in September, 1909. "Our sister is remembered by us for a unique brightness of spirit, queenly, sweet and winsome, and most devoted to the women of the Congo." Her "Life Scenes from Congo Land" could not be imitated by anyone, and shows us what impressions Divine love must have left of her upon forlorn hearts out there.

Raymond U. Spielman

Mr. Spielman went to the field in the spring of 1911, and died in December, 1912. Mr. Spielman was a successful soul-winner. He used to delight to fill his pockets with tracts and spend the day on the streets of New York button-holing men and lead-

ing them to Christ. He displayed great
energy in curing and selling snake skins
to help meet the expenses of his going to
the Congo.

Alva Stevenson

This man, who died outside our mission
was an earnest, indefatigable worker. His
spirit was peculiarly humble and sweet. He
understood the natives remarkably well
and got along with them finely. He never
spared himself, but plodded on for years
preaching far and near with great zeal. His
widow survives him.

Japan

Dr. James P. Ludlow

Dr. Ludlow, one of our pioneer missionaries, was born in South Carolina, in 1833.
With his wife he went to Japan in 1888, re-
maining in active and fruitful service till
1891. Our brother did a wide and varied
work through an interpreter, by preaching
and by Bible and tract distribution reaching with the Gospel all classes and conditions of both foreigners and Japanese. He
passed away in Seattle, Washington, May
7, 1898. Dr. Ludlow was a man of schol-

arly tastes and attainments, of exceptional ability, and of deep spirituality.

Hayti, West Indies
MRS. JULIA LANGLEY

Mrs. Julia Langley spent several years in missionary work under the Alliance on the island of Hayti at Port au Prince. Mrs. Langley was a converted Roman Catholic, and a woman of very decided convictions and principles and most earnest consecration. She returned to this country on account of broken health. The last months of her life were spent in the Faith Home of Mrs. Campbell, Brooklyn, where she was greatly respected and beloved, and left a profound impression of faith and godliness.

Alliance Leaders and Home Workers
ELLEN A. GRIFFIN

Nellie Griffin, as she was affectionately called, was born in Binghamton, New York. Left a half-orphan in early life with others dependent upon her, she developed those qualities of self-reliance and energy which afterwards became so prominent in her life. "At the age of fourteen she was teaching a public school, although almost all she herself knew was self-taught. She had a quick, penetrating and logical mind, and a good literary style, and in the last two years of her life became a most useful writer, having contributed to "Word, Work and World" a number of the most valuable articles on Home and City Missions. There was, indeed, material on hand for an interesting volume on the work of Dr. Judson, Jerry McAuley, the Howard Mission and other sketches."

Raised a Roman Catholic, Miss Griffin was converted by Mr. Sankey during the Moody and Sankey meetings in the Hippodrome in New York City in 1876. She at once engaged in City Mission work and led hundreds of souls to Christ. She was one of the first members of the Gospel Tabernacle and was perfectly healed of long-standing heart trouble. When Berachah Home was opened in 1884 she became one of the deaconesses, giving herself unreservedly to ministering to the sick and suffering. After a lingering illness she died from tuberculosis, February 18, 1887. She passed through a great spiritual conflict, but won a glorious victory of eternal peace. A strong sense of justice, supreme loyalty of heart to her convictions, absolute disinterestedness, unwavering faith, self-sacrificing love,— these were the predominant traits of Miss Griffin's character.

Rev. Robert Roden

Mr. Roden was one of the teachers in the Missionary Training Institute in the early days in New York City. He had been a Methodist minister. He was a scholar of high attainments and had fine literary taste. He was an excellent Bible teacher of thorough training and long experience. Spiritually, he was a man full of faith and the Holy Ghost. He diffused the savor of the knowledge of Christ, and his fragrant memory is a precious heritage.

Harriet A. Waterbury

Harriet Waterbury was a teacher in the Missionary Training Institute, in New York City, and also associate editor of our weekly paper. By birth and early training she was a Quakeress, and for some years was principal of a public school. Miss Waterbury was an exceptional teacher. Her courses in Bible Doctrine and Church History were among the strongest ever given in the Institute. Her work on the paper was of the highest order. She had the editorial instinct, and was an able and popular writer. She died in Berachah Home, in 1891. Harriet Waterbury had a strong personality and a gracious and winning manner, which attracted and won hosts of friends. Of her Dr. Wilson said: "And dear Miss Waterbury, than whom no truer heart ever beat in sympathy with the trials and triumphs of this Alliance work."

Henry W. Burnham

"On October 13, 1897, there entered into rest that sweet, simple-hearted man of God, tender as a woman and simple as a child in his faith, Mr. H. W. Burnham, of Kenwood, New York." For years Mr. Burnham was treasurer of our Society. He was a firm believer and staunch supporter of the Fourfold Gospel. In his last years he was a venerable figure, even patriarchal in appearance, and was highly respected and greatly beloved by all who knew him.

Rev. Charles N. Kinney

Charles N. Kinney, of Ossining, New

York, was for years president of the International Missionary Alliance. He really gave his life to the cause of missions, his daughter Helen in the early years having gone to Japan under our Board. He passed away in March, 1907. "No more simple-hearted child of God, no more prayerful spirit, no one with a clearer vision of Jesus, and of our calling and work in Him as an Alliance, no more generous giver, both according to, and beyond his means, no man more deeply loved by all who knew him, ever formed a part of our Society or held office among its members, than Charles N. Kinney." Mrs. Kinney, who died in 1897, was one of the oldest and truest friends of our work. Her life was greatly used of God and richly honored with His blessing.

JOHN CONLEY

John Conley was a princely merchant of Pittsburgh. He carried the spirit of business enterprise into the Lord's work. He was indeed a modern Barnabas. Mr. Conley founded our Palestine mission, and supported Miss Dunn's work there till the close of his life. At the same time his heart was in home missions. To him the coming of the Lord was a blessed and living hope. He was a member of the Board of Managers. He went to his reward July 25, 1897.

S. R. WILMOT

Mr. Wilmot was the first president of the International Missionary Alliance. In his home town, Bridgeport, Connecticut, he built the Berean Church, and his commodious home was the hospitable headquarters of the Lord's servants. He was a simple, unostentatious man, quiet and modest in demeanor and consecrated and self-sacrificing in spirit. From the wall of our Mission Room in New York Mr. Wilmot's kindly face looks down in inspiration and benediction. Our brother went to be with the Lord in 1897.

MAJOR OLIVER M. BROWN

Major Brown died at the Soldiers' Home, Sandusky, Ohio, November 25, 1910. "For many years his home has been at Beulah Park, where his venerable figure was always in evidence at the annual convention, as well as in all regular meetings. He was

eighty-five years of age at death. He was
an oak of Bashan or cedar of Lebanon,
flourishing in old age. To the chaplain of
the Home he remarked, when repeating the
text, 'I have fought a good fight, I have
kept the faith,' or 'rather,' said he with emphasis, 'the faith has kept me all these
years.' He was a veteran of the civil war.
He was the founder of the Faith Missionary Society, the founder of the Christian
Alliance of the State of Ohio, and for years
the president of the state organization of
our Society."

Thomas A. Cullen

Mr. Cullen met his death by drowning, in
Portland, Oregon, October 6, 1909. He was
district superintendent of the Northwest.
"He was in the full flush of early manhood,
not yet thirty-three years of age. Fifteen
years before he had been radically converted to God, and had given up all to Christ, to
be His missionary. In Peru he had served
in independent capacity for some years, until compelled to retire to this country tem-
porarily for his wife's sake. He had taken
high rank among us spiritually and in the

qualities of a safe, strong leader. God had done great things for him and his, so that the prospect was good of their returning soon to South America, when, in seeking to save his little child from drowning, he was engulfed himself, though a strong, practiced swimmer, in a treacherous place."

Mrs. M. S. Black

Mrs. Black, of Detroit, Michigan, who died July 9, 1909, was a liberal friend of our work. "She was a woman of great abilities, large possessions, but most consecrated, trustful, and peaceful, triumphant, spirtual in discernment, and generous though unobtrusive benevolence."

Mrs. O. E. Mallory

This Godly woman, the wife of the Rev. O. E. Mallory, one of the honorary vice-presidents of the Society, and the mother of Mrs. M. B. Fuller, of India, was remarkably healed in her earlier life and devoted her energies as a thanksliving to her God. Her children are her best memorial. She died in 1901.

Mrs. J. C. Crawford

Mrs. J. C. Crawford, wife of the superintendent of the Western district, who died

at Boone, Iowa, November 10, 1909, "was
a sweet and accomplished musican, devoting her talents to God's praise and the
training of young men and women, a woman of fragrant and winning spirit, peculiarly so to the young. No less than forty-
five young men and women appeared in her
Bible class the first Sunday after her departure to call her name blessed."

Dr. Amelia Barnett

This good woman, who died December
26, 1897, at the ripe age of eighty-four, may
be claimed not only by the Gospel Tabernacle but by the larger Alliance constituency. For years she was associated with
Dr. Lozier in the Woman's College of Medicine in New York City. She was a woman
of strong character and decided opinions,
yet of exalted Christian faith, and with a
heart full of sympathy and tenderness for
the sick and suffering. She was known as
the "Good Samaritan." For years Dr. Bar-
nett rendered invaluable assistance in Berachah Home as consultant. Although she
practiced medicine, yet, through her own
restoration from valvular heart disease, she
firmly believed in Divine Healing without

the use of means; and in cases where the mind of the Lord was clearly revealed, her simple faith and believing prayer were often instrumental in full restoration to health.

Mrs. Margaret J. Clark

"Mother Clark" had been an evangelist in the Methodist Church, and had labored with Mrs. Maggie Van Cott. After a remarkable healing from heart disease she joined the Alliance, and for a score of years was a familiar figure in the Gospel Tabernacle, New York, and at many of our larger eastern conventions. She loved the Fourfold Gospel and was an able and faithful witness to the power of the risen and glorified Christ to save and sanctify, to heal and satisfy. Mrs. Clark went to be with the Lord in 1906.

Rev. James Lyall

Although born in Scotland, Mr. Lyall came to this country when a youth and received his education at Oberlin College. At a Beulah Park Convention in the early days he came in touch with the Alliance, and was greatly blessed. He developed rare evangelistic gifts, and held meetings in various parts of the United States and throughout Great Britain. He made a tour of India, and following up the Torrey and Alexander campaign visited New Zealand and Australia, returning home richly rewarded in having been instrumental in the salvation of souls and in the deepening of the spiritual lives of believers. For a short time Mr. Lyall was a Field Superintendent of the Alliance. He died early in January, 1910, from anæmia, contracted while en route to India years before. "He was a man of distinct and noble pattern, strong in the Lord and strong for souls and the cause of Christ. His great themes were the reality and preciousness of the atoning blood, the personal, mighty Spirit, and the living Word of God. He was delightful in fellowship, and mighty in service, given to prayer and the ministry of the Word."

Rev. John E. Cookman, D.D.

John Cookman had an honored ancestry. His grandfather was a Wesleyan preacher in England, while his father, his brother Alfred, and he himself were ministers of the Methodist Episcopal Church. In this connection it may be added that his son is also a Methodist preacher.

Mr. Cookman's father, the Rev. George G. Cookman, was a man of commanding ability, who had a national reputation as an orator and was at one time chaplain of the United States Senate. He was lost at sea on the ill-fated steamer "President" in 1850. Mrs. Cookman was a very godly woman, of remarkable sweetness and strength of character. Of an older brother, Alfred Cookman, it may be truly said that he was one of the saints of the Christian church. A half century ago he was one of the most prominent advocates of holiness in the country. His dying testimony, in 1870, was: "I am sweeping through the gates, washed in the blood of the Lamb."

John was saved in Philadelphia, when a lad, in later years attributing his conversion to the faith and prayers of his mother and the example and influence of Alfred. Early in his Christian experience he made a profession of the Wesleyan doctrine of sanctification. With the exception of three years in Boston, his ministry of over a quarter of a century was spent in and near New York City. Mr. Cookman inherited from both parents a nervous temperament. Moreover, he had a weak heart, and for many years suffered intensely from insomnia and depression, several times breaking down from nervous prostration. After an unusually severe and prolonged attack of heart failure, he was remarkably healed in December, 1883. The Lord appeared to him in a vision, and said: "I am thy Healer, thy Sanctifier, thy Saviour, and thy Lord." Soon afterwards he became associated with Mr. Simpson in the work of the Alliance. Some little time before his death, which occurred in 1891, Mr. Cookman, for personal reasons, left the ministry of the Methodist Church and entered the priesthood of the Protestant Episcopal Church.

John Cookman was God's gift to the Alliance in the early years. For those who were associated with him no pen sketch is needed to refresh the memory, while to those who never knew or heard him no words can give an adequate impression of this unique man. East and west, north and south he toured the country with Mr. Simpson, not only glowingly proclaiming but radiantly exemplifying the glorious Gospel of the Fulness of Jesus. His distinguished family connections, his wide influence, his blameless walk, his eloquent lips, his safe and sane presentation of the Fourfold Gospel,—thes: various factors, combined with a gracious charm of personality and an Apostolic enduement of the Holy Ghost, clothed his public utterances with tremendous power. The fact is, the man was a veritable dynamo of spiritual energy. He seemed never to tire. He was indeed a "burning and a shining light." Of dear John Cookman his friends and associates may well say:

"Take him all in all, we ne'er shall see his like again."

Rev. David W. Le Lacheur

David Le Lacheur was of French Huguenot descent. He was born in Prince Edward's Island, in 1841. He gave his heart to the Lord when fourteen years of age. He was educated at Mount Allister College. Ordained as a Wesleyan preacher, he later became a Methodist minister and was a member of the Maine Conference. He was pastor at Lewiston, Hallowell, Biddeford, and at Pine Street, Portland. He organized an independent work in Portland, building the Vaughn Street Church, of which he was pastor for ten years.

Mr. Le Lacheur was a member of the Old Orchard Camp Meeting Association, on the grounds of which the Old Orchard Convention is held. In this way he became acquainted and later connected with the Alliance. Responding to a Divine call, in 1893 he went to Singapore, intending to engage in missionary work in the Philippine Islands; but the door being closed, he landed in China. Here he became the superintendent of our three missions, making some extraordinary tours, in one instance penetrating to the eastern borders of Thibet. Returning home in 1898, he was for two years Field Superintendent. In the fall of 1900 Mr. Le Lacheur undertook by request of the Board of Managers a deputational visitation of our missions in the Orient. He had been to Japan, China, the Philippine Islands, India, and had reached Palestine, whence the Board expected him to return direct to the Homeland. The needs of our African missions, however, strongly appealed to him. Consequently, against the better judgment of his associates on the Board and in an infirm state of health he went to Sierra Leone, to visit our Soudan Mission. He had scarcely reached Freetown, when in that torrid, deadly climate he was stricken with the aggravation of a chronic trouble. He fought bravely, but against too heavy odds. He died and was buried in Freetown, June 16, 1901.

Mr. Le Lacheur was an untiring worker,— a brave warrior and a faithful witness, as much as any martyr sealing his testimony with his life. He had a rugged, fearless nature, yet an attractive, winning personality. He was witty, good at repartee, and had a well developed sense of humor. Moreover, he had varied gifts: he was equally at home in giving a spiritual message from the pulpit and in delivering a missionary address on the platform. As a missionary pioneer on the confines of the Chinese Empire, he was intrepid; as a convention speaker, pleading the cause of the heathen world, he was magnetic; as a counsellor in the Board or on deputational visits he was wise; while in the closer and more intimate circles of friendship and affection he was loyal, tender, and loving.

Rev. Wilbur Fisk Meminger

Wilbur Meminger's father, the Rev. William McKean Meminger, of the Methodist Episcopal Chuch, is described as "an intellectual giant, a man of deep spirituality, a Hebrew, Greek and Latin scholar, ever ready to give his children instruction." His mother was Rebecca Watts, a charming Virginia woman, and a descendant of Isaac Watts, the hymn writer. The boy was born in Hedgesville, Va., April 29, 1851.

Wilbur received a good education, developing a rather extraordinary talent for oratory and elocution. When Fort Sumpter was fired on, the lad offered his services to the Union! Somewhat later he was again disappointed in his ambition to go to Annapolis. At the age of twenty-two he was converted in a Methodist revival.

Mr. Meminger entered business in Tyrone, Pennsylvania, and took an active part in church work, becoming in succession Sunday School teacher, steward, class leader, trustee, exhorter, local preacher, and finally Sunday School superintendent in the Methodist Church. It is enough to say that he filled each position with spiritual efficiency. Responding to a Divine call to preach, Mr. Meminger, while continuing in business, held evangelistic meetings in near by towns, being instrumental in the salvation of hundreds of souls. Through the ministry of Amanda Smith at Pitman Grove camp meeting he entered into the experience of "Perfect Love."

It was through a sentence in a letter from Stephen Merritt, reading, "I believe in the Fourfold Gospel," that Mr. Meminger first learned of the Alliance, whose teaching and testimony concerning the fulness of Jesus he soon thereafter heartily accepted. Indeed, he was made president of the new branch of our Society in his home town. This was in 1895. About this time he was compelled to abandon his evangelistic work on account of a bad throat, entailing loss of voice. This was a chronic trouble, the result of diphtheria in early life. But while attending an Alliance meeting in Altoona he was remarkably healed.

In 1897 Mr. Meminger was called to take

charge of the work of the Alliance in Chicago. Here he remained for three years. During this time he had an extraordinary ministry. The field was an exceptionally hard one. But he not only built up the work but extended its influence far and wide. Remarkable instances of conversion, remarkable cases of healing, in fact remarkable events along many lines were common occurrences. The man himself left his impress on the city, so that in later life he was glad to be known as "The little man from Chicago."

In 1900 our brother became Field Superintendent, for nine years going everywhere throughout the country extending the teaching and organizing the work of the Alliance. October 6, 1909, while addressing a street meeting near the Gospel Tabernacle, New York, he fell, and within a few minutes had gone to be with the Lord.

The life of Mr. Meminger, prepared by his widow, makes unnecessary any attempt at characterization. The man was not a type. He was in a class by himself. When the Lord made him, He broke the mould. Wilbur Meminger could have no successor.

Four things about him, however, may be recalled to mind. First, he was a living epistle. He believed the whole Gospel, and he exemplified the whole Gospel. Second, he was a thrilling speaker. He had extraordinary descriptive power. He could paint a scene with dramatic realism. Third, he was an original worker. He caught the spirit but did not follow the methods of the Salvation Army. To him the Lord was the Captain of our salvation; the believer was a soldier; and the Christian life was a warfare. Many of his field reports read like the telegraphic dispatches of a commanding general from the firing line of battle. And fourth, he was a man of prayer. He lived on his knees, and when he got hold of the horns of the altar of intercession things had to give way.

Mrs. Jennie Frow Fuller

Jennie Frow was born in Winchester, Ohio, December 16, 1851. She was converted in early life, and taught school when she was sixteen. At the age of nineteen she attended Normal School at Lebanon, Ohio. Here she gave her life wholly to God for any service He might have for her.

In 1873 Miss Frow entered Oberlin College, where under the strong influence of President Finney her religious views developed and her spiritual life ripened. Mr. Finney's teaching concerning the important place of the will in Christian experience profoundly impressed her. Later in her own ministry she made the will prominent in a holy walk. Miss Frow left Oberlin at the close of her junior year, and responding to a call from Albert Norton for reinforcements in 1876 sailed for India, where for three and a half years she labored at Ellichpur, in Berar. During the famine season of 1877-1878 she was active in relief work, and experienced many striking instances of Divine providence and answered prayer.

In 1880 Miss Frow returned to America on furlough, the following year becoming Mrs. M. B. Fuller, and in 1882 returning with her husband to Akola, Berar, where they had a fruitful ministry. The years 1890-1892 were spent by Mrs. Fuller in the homeland, her headquarters being at North Chili, New York, in a Free Methodist community. The time was spent in needed rest and in earnest advocacy of foreign missions. In 1892 Mr. and Mrs. Fuller became the superintendents of our Alliance mission in India, returning to the field with a large number of new missionaries, which by 1894 was swelled to sixty. It was in this year that the Gujerati field was opened. Bombay became the new headquarters. From here Mrs. Fuller made frequent and painstaking visitations to all the stations, establishing the work and strengthening the missionaries. Her work was of incalculable blessing.

In 1897 the death of little Jeannie Fuller, aged six, brought a great sorrow to her parents on the eve of their departure for the homeland. Here, however, they remained only a brief season, and were back on the field early in 1898. For the next two years Mrs. Fuller's labors were indefatigable, both for her missionary associates and for the famine sufferers. Indeed, her unselfish and unstinting service was shared by mission workers of other Boards. In the spring of 1900, while in a weakened condition from overwork, Mrs. Fuller was stricken with cholera. She lingered for thirteen weeks. For a time strong hope was entertained for her recovery; but heart and lung complications developed, and she passed to her eternal rest, June 21st. Her funeral service was widely representative of foreign and native religious interests in India, and memorial tributes appeared throughout the entire country as well as in England and America.

Mrs. Fuller was the best known and best loved missionary in Western India. Dr. Wilson called her "the woman apostle to the women of India." Indeed, this godly and gifted little woman's name is worthy to stand side by side with the name of any missionary in any country in any century. Higher or juster praise one could not give. A memorial volume, "A Life for God in India," has been prepared by Helen S. Dyer, of that country. But perhaps Mrs. Fuller's best memorial is her "Wrongs of Indian Womanhood," a missionary classic. Besides this she wrote a little book on "God's Care," a tract on "Convenant Promises to Parents," and was a frequent and valued contributor not only to our own Alliance Weekly, but also to the Bombay Guardian.

Rev. Henry Wilson, D.D.

Henry Wilson was born in Peterborough, Canada, April 20, 1841. His father was a master in one of the Canadian schools. Winning the Wellington Scholarship, he entered Trinity College, Toronto, from which he took several degrees, receiving the highest and last, that of Doctor of Divinity, in 1883. When he left college he was broken in health.

Entering the priesthood of the Church of England, Dr. Wilson became curate of the Cathedral of St. George's, in Kingston, Canada. Here and at the parish church in Cateraqui he had a successful ministry of seventeen years. During this time he passed through deep trial in the loss of both his first and second wives, and in the drowning of his only boy, a child of seven years.

"It was in Kingston that the great crisis and turning point in his life came. The Salvation Army up to that time was an unknown factor. On its arrival, despite his high churchly standing, he boldly and uncompromisingly stood up for its principles, defended its methods, answered its critics,

and later in life sealed his intense devotion
to its cause by giving his elder daughter to
its service. He was influenced to take .ais
step chiefly because at the mourners' bench
in one of the Army meetings he himself had
come into the experimental knowledge of
the Lord Jesus Christ as his Saviour. But
his attitude toward the Army cost him his
living. His Dean gave him his choice. He
made it, and leaving behind him the work
of seventeen years, a city full of heart-
broken friends, three lonely little graves in
a country churchyard (which church he
had labored for years to build for the people of that district, and where he now lies)
he went forth, not knowing whither he
went, taking with him his two motherless
little girls."

In 1884 Dr. Wilson became head assist-
ant of the clergy house of Saint George's
Episcopal Church, in New York, of which
Dr. W. S. Rainsford was rector. He was
instrumental in opening Avenue A Mission.
It was toward the close of his seven years'
ministry here that Dr. Wilson became associated with the Alliance. This was
through his healing in the old Twenty-third

Street Theater. From college days he had been the victim of chronic dyspepsia, catarrhal and throat trouble, and nervous depression, resulting in severe invalidism. But under the teaching of Mr. Simpson he was anointed and made a new man physically as a few years before he had been made a new man spiritually in Christ Jesus.

In 1891 Dr. Wilson became associate pastor of the Gospel Tabernacle. Here for ten years he had a blessed ministry. Besides being superintendent of the Sunday School he was for a time president of the International Missionary Alliance. In 1901 he became Field Superintendent. "His duties called him to spend at least half his time in long and often trying journeys in every part of the United States and Canada. He traveled tens of thousands of miles every year and visited scores of cities, towns, and villages from the Atlantic to the Pacific, and from Maine to Florida. Often he was exposed to inclement weather, railway breakdowns, damp and cold rooms, irregular living, and fatiguing labors. But he was always the same radiant and rejoicing example of the victorious life which he so beautifully portrayed." In a quick transition from Canada to the Southland he contracted a heavy cold; and while he was attending the Atlanta Convention double pneumonia developed, ending his life February 13, 1908.

"Henry Wilson, One of God's Best," is the title of a memorial volume prepared by his daughter and Mr. Simpson. It is sufficient here to recall to mind four traits of his personality and four phases of his ministry.

In appearance Dr. Wilson had a strong, noble face. "His form was stately, athletic, erect. His bearing was dignified and graceful. His dress, while distinctly clerical, was yet simple and unconventional. His manners were polished but affable, free and unaffected. He was at home in any circle. He was always a gentleman."

His scholarship was ripe and accurate. "His reading was of great range, especially along the lines of history, biography and the classics of general literature. He was a fine Greek and Latin scholar, and his Greek Testament was his constant companion."

Our brother was radiantly cheerful and

joyful. "It was a settled uplift of soul that had set its face toward the sunrising and refused to look on the dark side, to be soured by sensitiveness or suspicion or allow anything to cloud its sunshine or rob it of its victory." Blended with this sublime Christian optimism was a racial and personal gift of wit and humor, which, while always controlled by the Holy Spirit, enlivened his public address and made him a genial and charming companion.

Pre-eminently, Henry Wilson exemplified the life of the risen, glorified Christ. "The internal Christ" was the term he loved to use. Physically and mentally, as well as spiritually, his ready and glowing testimony was, "Christ liveth in me."

As a preacher, Dr. Wilson appealed to thoughtful minds, because he was intensely practical. He hated shams and held to a severe moral standard. Consistency was part of his very makeup. Moreover, he loved the lost and had a passion for souls. He was president of the Seaman's Christian Association and chaplain of the Magdalene Home at Inwood-on-Hudson.

As a counsellor, our brother was wise

and strong. He was an influential member
of the Board of Managers, and for years
secretary of the India Mission. He made
an important deputational visitation to
Sweden in connection with the outgoing of
a large company of missionaries from that
country under our Board.

As a writer, Dr. Wilson wielded a facile
and graceful pen. He had a cultured,
charming style. While he lived no one
else was thought of to write the memorial
paper for the Annual Council. Years ago
he prepared a series of scholarly articles on
"Veins of Truth from the Mines of God."
At the time of his death he had nearly ready
for publication material for a good sized
memorial volume containing sketches of
the lives of our deceased missionaries. He
had also collected a number of photographs
for the book. The writer hereby acknowledges his indebtedness to this incomplete
but painstaking and thorough work for the
conception, the plan and some of the material for this Appendix.

But it is in connection with his work for
the children that Dr. Wilson will live longest in memory and affection. Shall we call

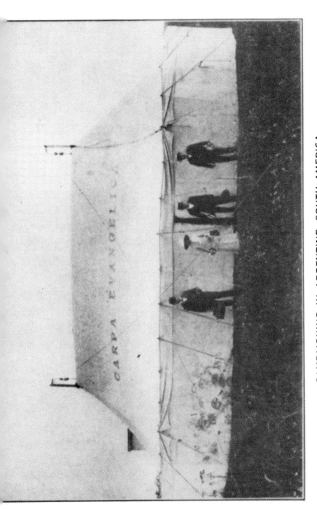

CAMPAIGNING IN ARGENTINE, SOUTH AMERICA.

him the apostle to children? Surely, we may, for he was their sympathizer and interpreter, their friend and lover. Not only the children of the Gospel Tabernacle and the entire Alliance, but the children of the whole world were on his heart. Five thousand children at home he enlisted in the support of 5,000 children in heathen lands, he himself assuming responsibility for 1,000. Every week for years he edited a Children's Page in the Alliance Weekly, under the initials "B. B. B." signifying "Big Baby Brother." Out of these weekly letters grew his book, "Bible Lamps for Little Feet."

Dr. John K. Smith

Dr. J. K. Smith, of Harrisburg, Pennsylvania, was for many years the President of the Eastern District of the Christian and Missionary Alliance, and until his death recognized as a beloved and honored leader in the Alliance work. Although a prominent physician, he took a decided stand for the doctrine of Divine Healing, and was a loyal witness to the teaching and work of the Alliance.

MARY GLOVER DAVIES.

Mary Glover Davies, of England, was another of our honored fellow-workers. She spent several years in the United States in intimate personal and official relations to the work, and was for two years one of our field evangelists. She was a strong character and a most effective platform speaker; and her sturdy and impressive eloquence made her a striking figure at our Alliance conventions. She returned to England in 1911 and the following year passed to her eternal reward.

JOSEPHUS L. PULIS

Mr. Pulis was one of the most impressive figures in all the history of the work. His earthly career closed in December, 1913. For more than thirty years he was intimately associated with the leaders of the movement. Indeed, he became attached to the personal work of Mr. Simpson years before the Alliance was formally organized and was one of the seven who met one cold November afternoon in the Caledonian Hall, Eighth Avenue, New York, to organize this humble movement. He was for years a member of the Board of Trustees,

and elder in the Gospel Tabernacle Church,
and the leader of the afternoon services in
Berachah Chapel, where he came into close
touch with hundreds of our people as they
visited the city. Mr. Pulis was a man of
strong personality, wonderfully saved, and
sanctified wholly, and filled with the Holy
Spirit, and the most consecrated and experienced Christians counted it a privilege to
sit at his feet and drink in the spirit and
teachings of the Master from His anointed
lips.

Mrs. M. L. Cassilly

One of the oldest friends and supporters
of the Alliance work was Mrs. M. L. Cas-
silly of East Forty-seventh Street, New
York City. She was attracted to the Tabernacle and the special services conducted
by Mr. Simpson away back in the eighties,
and until her death in the year 1905 was a
constant, and frequent, and generous supporter of the work. In the course of these
years she gave tens of thousands of dollars
to our missionary work and was a warm
friend of many of the missionaries and the
hostess of Mr. Le Lacheur and others during their furloughs.

SYDNEY M. WHITTEMORE

The late Sydney Whittemore was another of the early official workers of the Alliance. He was the first President of what was then known as the International Missionary Alliance, and his wife, who still survives him, Mrs. E. M. Whittemore, was for many years the Secretary and came into very close touch with the missionaries and the work during the first decade of its history. Mr. Whittemore was a prominent business man of New York City, and in his late years was honored by the rescue mission workers by his repeated election to the presidency of the Union of Mission Workers in the United States and Canada. He passed to his rest in February, 1914.

DR. A. J. GORDON

Dr. A. J. Gordon, of Boston, while not officially connected with the Christian and Missionary Alliance, was one of its warmest friends. He was a frequent speaker at our conventions and in the Gospel Tabernacle, New York, and an intimate friend of the leader of the work. He was in full sympathy with the Alliance testimony and special aims of its missionary work, and a number of his own students from the Boston Bible Training School became missionaries of the Society. It is needless to speak of his lofty character and noble life and service. His memory will always be cherished by the older workers of the Alliance, and his spirit often seems to hover over our assemblies along with John Cookman and Henry Wilson, the three most unique figures of all the history of these years.

F. L. CHAPELL

Second only to Dr. Gordon in the appreciation and love of our people was Dr. F. L. Chapell, who for nearly a score of years was in the closest and most active co-operation with our Alliance work. Dr. Chapell was attracted to the early meetings in connection with Divine Healing, and fully accepted the Alliance testimony on that subject. He was a remarkable Bible student and a profound interpreter of the Scriptures, especially of dispensational and prophetic truth. He became the superintendent of the Boston Bible Training School during his later years. He was almost always a prominent figure at our Old Orchard and other annual conventions and a frequent lecturer at the Missionary Training Institute, New York and Nyack.

Dr. James H. Brookes

One of the most prominent figures in advanced dispensational teaching a generation ago was Dr. James H. Brookes, of St. Louis, who at that time was an intimate friend of the founder of the Alliance. In later years he strongly opposed the doctrine of Divine Healing, but by a singular providence was led before the close of his life to embrace and bear public testimony to that truth, and the last two articles that he ever wrote were papers on the subject of Divine Healing under his name, published in the Christian and Missionary Alliance Weekly a few months before his death. It is a pleasure to bear testimony to this honored leader and his fellowship in the truth even to the last,

TITLES in THIS SERIES

geles, 1925), *AROUND THE WORLD BY FAITH, WITH ... WEEKS IN THE HOLY LAND* (Los Angeles, n. d.), *T... YEARS MISSION WORK IN EUROPE JUST BEFORE T... WORLD WAR, 1912-14* (Los Angeles, [1926])

6. Boardman, W. E., *THE HIGHER CHRISTIAN L... (Boston, 1858)

7. Girvin, E. A., *PHINEAS F. BRESEE: A PRINCE IN ISR/...* (Kansas City, Mo., [1916])

8. Brooks, John P., *THE DIVINE CHURCH* (Columb... Mo., 1891)

9. RUSSELL KELSO CARTER ON "FAITH HEALIN... R. Kelso Carter, *THE ATONEMENT FOR SIN AND SI... NESS* (Boston, 1884) *"FAITH HEALING" REVIEW... AFTER TWENTY YEARS* (Boston, 1897)

10. Daniels, W. H., *DR. CULLIS AND HIS WORK* (Bosto... [1885])

11. HOLINESS TRACTS DEFENDING THE MINISTRY... WOMEN. Luther Lee, *"WOMAN'S RIGHT TO PREA... THE GOSPEL; A SERMON, AT THE ORDINATION OF RE... MISS ANTOINETTE L. BROWN, AT SOUTH BUTLE... WAYNE COUNTY, N. Y., SEPT. 15, 1853"* (Syracus... 1853) *bound with* B. T. Roberts, *ORDAINING WOM... (Rochester, 1891) *bound with* Catherine (Mumfor... Booth, *"FEMALE MINISTRY; OR, WOMAN'S RIGHT ... PREACH THE GOSPEL . . ."* (London, n. d.) *bou... with* Fannie (McDowell) Hunter, *WOMEN PREAC... ERS* (Dallas, 1905)

12. LATE NINETEENTH CENTURY REVIVALIST TEACHIN... ON THE HOLY SPIRIT. D. L. Moody, *SECRET POW... OR THE SECRET OF SUCCESS IN CHRISTIAN LIFE AN...*

WORK (New York, [1881]) *bound with* J. Wilbur Chapman, RECEIVED YE THE HOLY GHOST? (New York, [1894]) *bound with* R. A. Torrey, THE BAPTISM WITH THE HOLY SPIRIT (New York, 1895 & 1897)

3. SEVEN "JESUS ONLY" TRACTS. Andrew D. Urshan, THE DOCTRINE OF THE NEW BIRTH, OR, THE PERFECT WAY TO ETERNAL LIFE (Cochrane, Wis., 1921) *bound with* Andrew Urshan, THE ALMIGHTY GOD IN THE LORD JESUS CHRIST (Los Angeles, 1919) *bound with* Frank J. Ewart, THE REVELATION OF JESUS CHRIST (St. Louis, n. d.) *bound with* G. T. Haywood, THE BIRTH OF THE SPIRIT IN THE DAYS OF THE APOSTLES (Indianapolis, n. d.) DIVINE NAMES AND TITLES OF JEHOVAH (Indianapolis, n. d.) THE FINEST OF THE WHEAT (Indianapolis, n. d.) THE VICTIM OF THE FLAMING SWORD (Indianapolis, n. d.)

4. THREE EARLY PENTECOSTAL TRACTS. D. Wesley Myland, THE LATTER RAIN COVENANT AND PENTECOSTAL POWER (Chicago, 1910) *bound with* G. F. Taylor, THE SPIRIT AND THE BRIDE (n. p., [1907?]) *bound with* B. F. Laurence, THE APOSTOLIC FAITH RESTORED (St. Louis, 1916)

5. Fairchild, James H., OBERLIN: THE COLONY AND THE COLLEGE, 1833-1883 (Oberlin, 1883)

6. Figgis, John B., KESWICK FROM WITHIN (London, [1914])

7. Finney, Charles G., LECTURES TO PROFESSING CHRISTIANS (New York, 1837)

8. Fleisch, Paul, DIE MODERNE GEMEINSCHAFTSBEWEGUNG IN DEUTSCHLAND (Leipzig, 1912)

19. SIX TRACTS BY W. B. GODBEY. *SPIRITUAL GIFTS A* *GRACES* (Cincinnati, [1895]) *THE RETURN OF JES* (Cincinnati, [1899?]) *WORK OF THE HOLY SPI* (Louisville, [1902]) *CHURCH—BRIDE—KINGD* (Cincinnati, [1905]) *DIVINE HEALING* (Greensbo [1909]) *TONGUE MOVEMENT, SATANIC* (Zarepha N. J., 1918)

20. Gordon, Earnest B., *ADONIRAM JUDSON GORD* (New York, [1896])

21. Hills, A. M., *HOLINESS AND POWER FOR THE CHUR AND THE MINISTRY* (Cincinnati, [1897])

22. Horner, Ralph C., *FROM THE ALTAR TO THE UPI ROOM* (Toronto, [1891])

23. McDonald, William and John E. Searles, *THE L OF REV. JOHN S. INSKIP* (Boston, [1885])

24. LaBerge, Agnes N. O., *WHAT GOD HATH WROUG* (Chicago, n. d.)

25. Lee, Luther, *AUTOBIOGRAPHY OF THE REV. LUTH LEE* (New York, 1882)

26. McLean, A. and J. W. Easton, *PENUEL; OR, FACE FACE WITH GOD* (New York, 1869)

27. McPherson, Aimee Semple, *THIS IS THAT: PI SONAL EXPERIENCES SERMONS AND WRITINGS* (L Angeles, [1919])

28. Mahan, Asa, *OUT OF DARKNESS INTO LIG* (London, 1877)

29. THE LIFE AND TEACHING OF CARRIE JUI MONTGOMERY Carrie Judd Montgomery, *"UND HIS WINGS": THE STORY OF MY LIFE* (Oaklan

[1936]) Carrie F. Judd, THE PRAYER OF FAITH (New York, 1880)

THE DEVOTIONAL WRITINGS OF PHOEBE PALMER Phoebe Palmer, THE WAY OF HOLINESS (52nd ed., New York, 1867) FAITH AND ITS EFFECTS (27th ed., New York, n. d., orig. pub. 1854)

Wheatley, Richard, THE LIFE AND LETTERS OF MRS. PHOEBE PALMER (New York, 1881)

Palmer, Phoebe, ed., PIONEER EXPERIENCES (New York, 1868)

Palmer, Phoebe, THE PROMISE OF THE FATHER (Boston, 1859)

Pardington, G. P., TWENTY-FIVE WONDERFUL YEARS, 1889-1914: A POPULAR SKETCH OF THE CHRISTIAN AND MISSIONARY ALLIANCE (New York, [1914])

Parham, Sarah E., THE LIFE OF CHARLES F. PARHAM, FOUNDER OF THE APOSTOLIC FAITH MOVEMENT (Joplin, [1930])

THE SERMONS OF CHARLES F. PARHAM. Charles F. Parham, A VOICE CRYING IN THE WILDERNESS (4th ed., Baxter Springs, Kan., 1944, orig. pub. 1902) THE EVERLASTING GOSPEL (n.p., n.d., orig. pub. 1911)

Pierson, Arthur Tappan, FORWARD MOVEMENTS OF THE LAST HALF CENTURY (New York, 1905)

PROCEEDINGS OF HOLINESS CONFERENCES, HELD AT CINCINNATI, NOVEMBER 26TH, 1877, AND AT NEW YORK, DECEMBER 17TH, 1877 (Philadelphia, 1878)

RECORD OF THE CONVENTION FOR THE PROMOTION OF

SCRIPTURAL HOLINESS HELD AT BRIGHTON, M
29TH, TO JUNE 7TH, 1875 (Brighton, [1896?])

40. Rees, Seth Cook, MIRACLES IN THE SLUMS (Chica
[1905?])

41. Roberts, B. T., WHY ANOTHER SECT (Rochest
1879)

42. Shaw, S. B., ed., ECHOES OF THE GENERAL HOLINE
ASSEMBLY (Chicago, [1901])

43. THE DEVOTIONAL WRITINGS OF ROBERT PEARSA
SMITH AND HANNAH WHITALL SMITH. [R]ob
[P]earsall [S]mith, HOLINESS THROUGH FAITH: LIG
ON THE WAY OF HOLINESS (New York, [1870]) [H]a
nah [W]hitall [S]mith, THE CHRISTIAN'S SECRET O
HAPPY LIFE, (Boston and Chicago, [1885])

44. [S]mith, [H]annah [W]hitall, THE UNSELFISHNE
OF GOD AND HOW I DISCOVERED IT (New Yor
[1903])

45. Steele, Daniel, A SUBSTITUTE FOR HOLINESS; c
ANTINOMIANISM REVIVED (Chicago and Bosto
[1899])

46. Tomlinson, A. J., THE LAST GREAT CONFLI
(Cleveland, 1913)

47. Upham, Thomas C., THE LIFE OF FAITH (Bosto
1845)

48. Washburn, Josephine M., HISTORY AND REMINI
CENCES OF THE HOLINESS CHURCH WORK IN SOUT
ERN CALIFORNIA AND ARIZONA (South Pasaden
[1912?])